BEYOND THE CATTLE GATE

Outlaw History, Legends, and Treasures

TIMOTHY DRAPER

WOLFPACK
PUBLISHING
— EST 2013 —

BEYOND THE CATTLE GATE

Acknowledgments

I'm dedicating this book to my father-in-law, Dean Dopp, who passed away as I was writing it. He was a good man who loved his family and enjoyed the old western culture. He was from the last generation that grew up hearing stories of cattlemen on wide open ranges, ruthless outlaw activities, and the mining era that changed the course of America. He heard many stories firsthand from his parents and grandparents. This book is for you, Dean. We'll see each other again—and don't worry, I'll take good care of your daughter.

I also want to acknowledge the people who lived in the era of big dreams and unexplored territories and possessed the bravery to conquer and withstand the unknown future. The West was wild and untamed. This posed a threat for every single man, woman, child, and family that traveled from east to west.

These stories you're about to read are based on actual events, documented by many throughout the years. You're going to learn about the historical accounts of the west and the outlaws that robbed themselves right into the history books.

We should also remember the men and women that protected others under the law and the heroes that fought for what they thought was right.

I want you to consider something as you press forward into this book. The cultural behaviors in this time period were vastly different than today. It was called the wild west for a reason. It was a much rougher and more challenging way of life in every respect imaginable. Many brave people took the law into their own hands, and were sometimes forced to do so. These are their stories.

Thank you to all the people who have been in my life and have shared so many adventures with me. I would like to thank my wife LeeAnn for being supportive as my journey continues to unfold. I couldn't do what I do without the inspiration of your presence, and that of our children.

Introduction

Get ready to step back in time and discover some of the most amazing untold history and information about the "wild west." It was a time of great change and upheaval in the U.S., and for many, it was considered a good move to step into the new frontier and try modernizing and taming the west. Some people, whether known to them or not, lived a dangerous lifestyle hurling them towards an unforeseen future.

This book will explain a pattern of life-changing events which occurred to form the wild west into a greedy place ripe for looting. Outlaws took advantage of the lawless land and carried on their robberies and murders for nearly a hundred years. If one outlaw or gang was caught and hung, another would soon show up and carry on where the others left off.

However, not all outlaws were what you have been told. Some of them were murderers and thieves. Some of them felt their actions were justified because of acts committed during the Civil War. Some of them fought against the Union, while others just plainly wanted to be bad. As the west grew and expanded, crime did, too, and this was a perfect recipe for lost treasures and hidden caches all over the western states. It was also the perfect time for pride, culture, and change.

Treasures can be found today if you know where to look and can figure out how they got there. In this book, I'll explain and give locations to the booming towns from the 1800s. You'll also learn about the main travel and getaway routes where so many unmarked graves can still be found today. I go into detail about the mining camps that turned into prosperous towns. I'll open your mind to the possibility that history has been suppressed and lost treasures are still hidden today. I'll also explain that the history you have read in the past, is only a summary of the old west. There's always more to the story.

To learn and understand this history, you'll need to be willing to accept new information and untold historical accounts. You'll also have to do your own research and get into the state of mind of these outlaws. Only then will you be able to see what I see when I look at the mountain ranges and open fields. I see opportunities and untold possibilities. I also see that our Nation's history is wrong in many respects, and that provides the motivation behind changing its stories.

You'll also need one more thing that I can only try to inspire you to—you'll have to be willing to go beyond the cattle gate to find this rich lost history. You'll have to become an avid adventurer on your own journey. Only then will you fully understand the old west and discover its lost secrets for yourself.

ONE

How the West Was Created

The great wide-open fields and mountains of the western United States captured the dreams of so many people and delivered possibilities for a better life many never expected to have. Open spaces were up for the taking, and many wanted the same thing that their ancestors came to the new world for: land. The idea of new towns and cities were a whisper in the eastern half of the country. Exploring an untamed world was a topic that many talked about. Some thought it was too far-fetched while others couldn't let it pass them by. The big city life in New York and other eastern cities wasn't necessarily what some envisioned as the perfect life.

Many people came from all over the world to escape the boundaries of a common, ordinary life. Many found themselves in parts of big eastern cities, poor and looking for work. The big city life wasn't exactly what they'd hoped for. Feces and garbage could be found every day on the streets. Homeless people slept wherever they could find a place. So many people were fighting over a few dollars every month to survive. Only the rich lived a life to admire. Hearing about miles and miles of free land started to sound good to some of the more daring souls. But, like so many things in life, nothing was free, and a price had to be paid. During this era, many paid with their own blood and heartache.

Let's take a step back even further in time than the 1890s. Let's go back about forty years more to the 1850s, to the time when the west was starting to expand. The United States was growing. The U.S. resident count was over twenty-three million people, according to 1850 Census records. That's almost a forty percent increase from ten years prior in 1840. America was growing, there was no doubt about that, and with that growth there was good and bad to the mix into the equation. For a few generations, people from around the world had wanted to live in America. Many people dreamed of owning their own land so they could live the farming life to support their families. Land meant power in those days, and it also stood for freedom.

Freedom to do what they wanted with their land coupled with the hopes of getting away from greedy landowners was key. For many years, places like England, Scotland, and Ireland were ruled by kings and queens. Noblemen and wealthy landowners. Many families were renting a small patch of land from these types of people and things were rarely in their favor. Rent on lands was increasing to sums that most could not afford. If rent wasn't paid, families would be pushed off their land and all their belongings taken away as payment. Homes were taken. Their livestock and food sources were just gone, in a matter of a few days. These families had nothing if this happened to them, leaving many in a state of utter desperation.

Talk of the new world, the United States of America, was reaching far flung places around the globe. The name became more than a word. The name itself was becoming a phase of power, hope, and freedom. As time went on, more and more people fell onto hard times under the belt of someone more powerful than them. In later years, people started to fight back for what they believed was right. It was called "The Rebellion." During this time, ships were leaving the shores of Europe and sailing to America, full of people and supplies. Yet again, though, many people could not afford to relocate their families.

Most people had grown up in their homelands for generations. It was not an easy task to consider, but many started to make preparations for their journey. Some families sold everything they owned to sail the seas to freedom. Some were more fortunate than others, and they not only bought their tickets, but were able to take things like family heirlooms and other items of importance. For some, they and their families never could leave their homes. Those classes of people were left to manage the best they could under the unwanted laws of the land.

For those that did leave, some of their dreams come true and some were faced with, even more, the realization that not all things were quite as they seemed. Not to mention those that left their family homes without their wife or kids. Too many people to count did leave and never saw their kin again. There were grandparents, uncles, aunts, and siblings who would never set eyes on them again in this life.

There was a brave new world in front of them, but there was also a sad old world behind them. Life at sea was hard enough. If you had enough money, some ships would treat you as a guest at a hotel. Many people spent days on end on the lower levels and used buckets for bathrooms. Disease and poor health usually came with the harsh, uncleanliness of these ships. I can only imagine that they felt they were making the right decision, despite the hardship. Once they landed in the ports of America, after days and days on the Atlantic Ocean, the dream of opportunity wasn't exactly spelled out to some foreigners.

Some arrived in America to find that things would be harder to accomplish than they'd been led to believe. Many were getting low on money and finding a good place to stay in these large cities wasn't easy. The open range was still a thousand or more miles away from these ports of entry. Horses and wagons would be needed, and if you were low on money, you would have to stay in the big cities and find work to pay for your travel. This is where it seemed to be hard for the foreigners once again. Instead of getting off the ship and walking down the sidewalk to your dreams waiting for you, you had to wait.

The right time would eventually come, but for most, that was much longer than they had initially hoped for. Looking for work wasn't easy, either. Many had to survive long enough to be lucky to find work and when they did, the pay didn't amount to much. Some of these jobs required very hard labor. Some jobs required women to turn to prostitution. Even worse, some had to turn to a life of thievery. Not many were able to rob their way to riches in the big city. It was more low-scaled pocket thieves and similar, just to make enough to eat each day.

The point is that making anywhere from nine to thirteen dollars a month prolonged their dream of heading west to claim their future. Some did succeed in making their way to the west and some didn't. The ones that were fortunate were able to find work that traveled to the west, such as jobs with the Union Pacific Railroad or hauling supplies from one city to the next. Some saved enough money and bought their horses and wagons. In this case, their dreams and hard work were still waiting for them. Traveling west in the old days wasn't an easy task. It wasn't just the long journey, it was what would hide in the shadows, waiting to emerge at the right moment. For some, it was the wrong moment.

Just as photography was invented—New York City, New York—1850

This type of expansion created money flow by way of transfer of payroll caches. This is where the bad and the desperate found their targets, robbing others. Back to the travel of heading west, many eastern states had somewhat safer roads to travel, but as soon as a person cleared the big cities and found themselves traveling the start of the Oregon Trail, the risk grew ten times greater. Because the railroad was under construction, even the rich had to travel the same way as the poor, riding by horse, horse-drawn carriage or wagon, or on foot. The Union Pacific Railroad started in Boston and moved its way to the west, but workers only managed to lay about 3 miles of track per day on average.

The thing is, traveling on foot, by horse, or by wagon would only allow a group to travel anywhere from eight to twenty miles a day. The trip from New York to the start of the Oregon Trail was around one thousand two hundred miles. Estimating that one could only travel ten miles a day, it would take around a hundred and twenty days.

That's not including time to rest, to fix a broken part on a wagon, or for any sickness or other trouble that may have slowed them down. This was a massive commitment, to say the least. For the lucky ones—those who weren't killed by bandits, by sickness, or even hostile Indians—that landed in Kansas City (the starting point of the Oregon Trail), they had only begun another journey. Kansas City was a good resting point and a place to regroup and gather supplies and restore money flow to continue forward.

It wasn't the safest part of the U.S. at the time; in fact, it was the opening to the gates of hell in the west. Gunfighters and bandits seemed to run the place. The law would prove to have a hard time keeping crime in check. Some people were able to press on as others took new jobs to save for the rest of their trip. This was a place that many called home as they never headed further west. The town was growing, and as I mentioned before, with growth and expansion comes crime and thieves. Stagecoaches and supplies were frequently entering town, and as far as the eye could see, there was nothing around. Nothing but hills, fields, and distant mountain ranges. This was a great place for outlaws and criminals to stay and stage their criminal operations from.

These bandits would take any chance they could. They would sometimes be seen in town while they sought out their next victims. Sometimes they would be spotted on the outskirts of town. Oftentimes these bandits were on the run. Some of them stayed local while some would go from town to town so the law couldn't easily track them. It's for this reason that Kansas City is a place of significant interest for buried caches and hidden treasures. Some of the bandits spent their newly stolen money in town and some would bury their treasure out in the wilderness. Some bandits were caught and hung, and some were shot by posses a few hours after they'd hidden their stolen loot in a cave or other hard to access spot. Sometimes they themselves were attacked and killed by hostile Indians, only to have their bodies found rotting on the ground. No one was safe in those days. No one. This was the vicious circle of life.

The possibilities are endless when it comes to the treasures of the old west. We'll save this part for later in the book when I'll go into further detail. The west was wild, no doubt about it, but you must picture something—people back in the 1800s were just like you and me. Hopes and dreams, work and money—everything that you want today, they wanted back then, too. Everything you hope for, they hoped for. Times are different, but the likes and dislikes of people have not changed. Remember that for later. If a person or group was lucky enough to head west, there were a few bigger cities emerging, rife with possibilities. A few of them were New Orleans, Louisiana; Mobile, Alabama; and St. Louis, Missouri, but many places were still small and untamed in the further western states.

That is until the gold rush of California, Nevada, and Alaska got started. The gold rush formed the western states of America, without a doubt. It created possibilities that raised an eyebrow or two. Small mining camps started to flourish, and many people were flooding these parts very quickly. Before anyone could blink, the talk of going west for gold was like people in the east talking about land. The gold rush and silver towns were a big reason why big cities now exist in the west—cities like Los Angeles, Phoenix, and more are now suburbs of these once thriving mining camps. The mining era brought many people to the area, and many people who weren't miners suddenly became eager to learn the trade. Businesses were started and many did well. However, the fact is only about three percent of miners actually struck it *rich* rich.

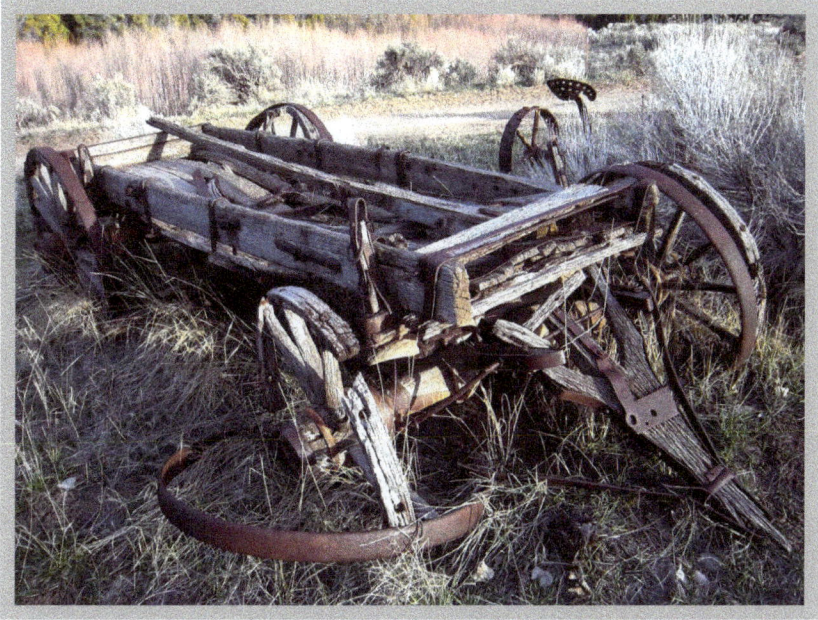

Old wagon from the Old Spanish Trail in Southern Utah

Many people worked for large mining companies that were successful, and the entrepreneurs who owned those ventures benefitted greatly from the dreams of others—and from their back-breaking labor, too. Stores, saloons, and hotels flourished. Sadly, the outlaws and bandits were good for business, too. They would rob stagecoaches and spend days in a town, drinking and spending money on women all manner of vice. Yep, things were looking good for the west. The Transcontinental Railroad was underway, building its railroad tracks from California to northern Utah. Meanwhile, stagecoaches and wagons were more in demand than ever.

This was the only way to move gold, silver, money, and

supplies prior to rail lines being completed. Now that the west was starting to boom, stagecoaches were reported in some towns every day, and oftentimes more than one. This is where the outlaws made off with a lot of valuables. The newly contracted and hired Pinkerton organization was created and placed in charge of protecting the cargo and that's where the saying "I'm riding shot-gun" comes from. Riding shotgun literally means sitting beside the coach driver, holding a shotgun, and being on the lookout for dangerous men. The Pinkerton National Detective Agency was started in Chicago in 1850 and was a private police force to help enforce the laws of the land. Not only would they travel with wagons full of valuables, but they would also track down and hunt after known outlaws. This helped local sheriffs and marshals out west.

Some mining camps and towns were plotted and built overnight in some of the rich mining areas. Sometimes a mining camp would sit there lawless until a sheriff was appointed. These types of camps became ripe targets for outlaws, and many times it took a tough, strong, and ruthless sheriff to take control of a town. Sometimes the sheriff appointed was aggressive enough, and sometimes the sheriff was murdered and would take a month or more to find another appointed sheriff to gain control of the town. Every town and mining camp was different. Some were safer places to live and some were extremely rowdy and full of crime. But it wasn't just mining camps being constructed in the west; there were suburbs starting to be built, as well.

These suburbs were created out of the need for checkpoints and resting towns. As mining was booming so quickly, the need for everything imaginable was being considered, and ways to provide these needs were being set in place. Traveling by wagons or horses caused a slowdown in the travel time. Many travelers set up camp in the wilderness next to a waterhole to rest and to let their horses have a couple of days' break. This is where a group could stay for a few days and do some food gathering and hunting. This is where anything living would replenish its energy and nutrition. The small towns along the known trails catered to these travelers. Hotels, restaurants, and stores were a big necessity, and the more people passed through these towns, the more business thrived.

Supply and demand were the keys to this way of living. If there were rich mines nearby, that would cause more attention to the growth patterns. In fact, if we move forward to the time when the railroad companies were completing their tracks—let's say the 1860s—many rich mining towns erected train tracks right through town and to the mines themselves. This changed a lot when it came to growth and how fast supplies, workers, and materials could come in and out of a town. This was the golden age for the western towns and states, and it brought even more people into the west. The old ways of life were beginning to see modernization.

Many mining towns started to boom as the price of gold and silver was high. Towns initially made up of canvas tents started to build wooden buildings. Churches, stores, hotels, and more were getting rid of the tent-style buildings, and construction workers started to build what we see today in ghost towns—old buildings with boardwalks that connect buildings throughout the town. The west was growing strong, but this created a whole new problematic situation—crime, outlaws, robberies, and murders.

Some people ask me how I know that treasures from the 1800s are still out there, buried or hidden. I tell everyone to learn your history because it's a game changer. Once you truly understand why people behaved the way they did and understand the value in cargo, gold, silver, and payroll, then you can understand why the valuables were coming in and out of these areas.

Once you learn about the outlaws and what they targeted, then you can see the wants and needs of their lifestyle. Lastly, once you understand and know the activities of the outlaws and where their stolen goods went, you can then truly understand that there are many treasures in these western states waiting for someone to uncover them. I want you to ponder on this as we move into a new chapter: did the bad guys always get away free and clear of trouble? Did they spend their stolen money? Were some of them chased by a posse, and in a panic, stash their valuables somewhere out of town for a clean get-away? If you answered yes to any of these questions, you're getting closer to understanding why treasures can still be found today.

I only asked you to consider three questions, and I know I could ask you many more. For now, this is a good start to understanding how to learn historical events and track down the lost history and hidden valuables that I know are still out there for the taking. Many of these treasures from train robberies, stagecoach hold-ups, bank lootings, and more have never been found or declared discovered. Even with modern-day equipment, a person would have a hard time tracking them down. You need to know the history of the area to start looking for treasures. I'm going to help provide these types of information and knowledge. Let's move on to more history and information, as we go further in-depth with the lives of Cow Boys, cattlemen, miners, farmers, outlaws, and more.

TWO

Wildest Towns in America

In the early Spring of 1865, the Civil War was ended, and people tried to move on from that type of life. The war lasted just over four years, but not everyone was ready to end it. In many ways, I don't think a lot of soldiers came back from the war with the mindset of moving on. How could they? Many people's lives were taken and so many families learned to move on without a husband, father, neighbor, and more. Most of these men that did come home were broken, and not just in a financial way. Some people said that their loved ones never made it home, even when that family member was sitting in a chair on the front porch. Some couldn't escape the memories and trauma that they experienced from the war.

Have you heard the story of the Hatfields and McCoys? It's a perfect situation that explains what I'm talking about with the war not ending for everyone. Both families fought for the Confederates, but this didn't stop bad feelings towards one another from developing. The Hatfields were starting to prosper in some businesses after the war and the McCoys saw this as a downfall. Randolph "Ole Ran'L" McCoy claimed that William Anderson Hatfield, better known as "Devil Anse," was a traitor to the Confederates due to his abandoning the war early. By the time Randolph McCoy returned home after his squadron was killed, he noticed that the Hatfields were in the logging business. This caused more hardship for the two families because of the dispute on which family owned the rights to the timbers.

I found some people would carefully say that some type of jealousy and animosity was starting to grow more and more towards the Hatfields because of their success. Several murders were committed by both families, and both sides lost loved ones. It was a vicious cycle of tension that lasted more than thirty years. It wasn't until more modern days that these two families decided a treaty should be made. This is just an example of two families and how the war may have affected the men.

Some say it was a bad tension from the start and some would disagree and say it was the war that changed their behaviors. Another thing that happened just before the war was over was something that may have changed the U.S. forever. Abraham Lincoln was assassinated, and that caused even more tension in the already divided country in 1865. From my research, some men came home bitter and still indecisive about the opposing side in the war, just like the story of the Hatfields and McCoys. I think it is safe to say that our country was sort of managing where and what the next steps were to better the country.

Despite the good and bad during this era, there were some that were more fortunate and ready to take on new ventures in the United States. Some people's ambitions were far more than others. Especially the powerful and wealthy people that owned large businesses. I'm now talking about the railroad companies. The shareholders and investors of these railroad companies were some of the richest in the United States. They had a dream to combine the east to the west coast with the tracks that kept the iron horse moving forward. The race was on with two train companies—The Transcontinental Railroad and the Union Pacific Railroad. These railroad companies had over three thousand miles of tracks to build. Many temporary work camps and towns were constructed all along their routes.

These towns served as sleeping quarters for the workers and

suppliers. Some had a church, brothels, saloons, and stores. These were towns made of canvas and when the railroad tracks moved down too far away from these towns, most of them broke down their tents and moved with the flow of work. The railroad tracks were close by to the more permanent towns and they deemed themselves useful for the growth of America. Unfortunately, the two railroad companies were conducting a race and competing at the time as they were paid by the mile.

For every mile that was laid down by the Union Pacific, they made money. The more tracks that were constructed, the more money was paid out. Both railroads were in a hurry to out earn the other. The Union Pacific started on the east coast and the Transcontinental Railroad started on the west coast. The plan was for both to meet in Utah around the same time. Both government contracts paid a different price for each mile of track. The eastern states were flat and full of fields while the west coast had mountain passes and solid rock to blast through. Without a doubt, the Union Pacific laid more tracks, but the Transcontinental Railroad was paid more generously.

Both railroads were hiring every man that they could find to finish this race. The bad part is that this created a mixture of hard-working men that were honest working family men with outlaws and bandits that didn't live according to the same values. Diversity was in the air, but unfortunately, the time for murder and robberies was on the rise. An outlaw (criminal) could get a job with the railroad companies, and very quickly disappear in the west without any consequences for their past wrongdoing. This was the starting point for known criminals to go where nothing could stop their way of life. A lawless future was in their path ahead.

Some of these criminals worked for the railroad long enough to disappear and somewhat blend in with other people in the west until they didn't. Murders and robberies were on the rise and the law had a hard time keeping the peace. Stagecoaches were robbed. Railroad payrolls were taken at gunpoint, and normal working people were shot in the streets for what was in their pockets. No one was safe. Some historical records show and talk about murders every day. Some towns were quieter, but that wouldn't last very long, not until the law could set a presence there. Even that wasn't enough as crime continued to flourish and outlaw gangs were created.

As the railroad companies finished more tracks, passenger cars on the trains were put to use. The trains granted a faster and easier way to travel to the west. It worked both ways. People from the west were able to travel to the east. Even though the two railroads hadn't connected yet, the opportunity was there.

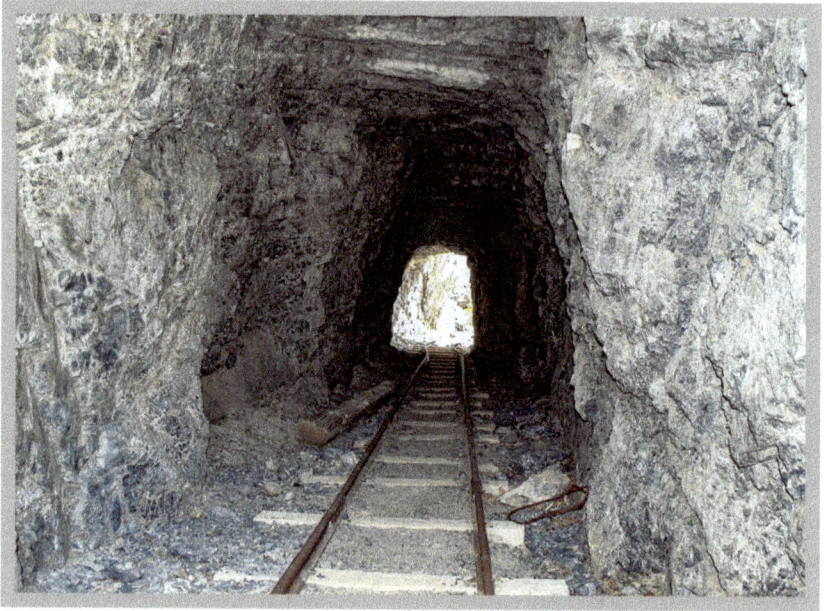

Many train tunnels can be found in the Western states.

Let's fast forward a few more years to the end of the 1860s, when many towns have already started a name for themselves. Let's take Pioche, Nevada, for starters. It was named "The Most Deadliest Town" in all of Nevada. Some say it was the worst in the western states. Pioche was founded in 1868, or at least it was declared a town during this time. This will give you an example of how wild the west was. Seventy-two people were murdered in Pioche before a single person in town died of natural causes. You had to be rough and tough and even that wasn't enough. There was always someone meaner and quicker to kill out there, no matter what.

Downtown Pioche, Nevada—1906

Pioche developed over five million dollars in silver within its first year. More discoveries of silver ore were located in the area and the town grew to six thousand residents. Gunfights were very common. Pioche became a place where many good people found it easy to live. According to history, it was a rough place to live. Outlaws started running out of control while the growth of the town was still booming. Law enforcement couldn't match the evil of these non-law-abiding citizens. Word of money and silver attracted the worst outlaws. They saw the town as an easy mark.

Miners were being robbed, right from their own mine entrance. Bandits found that these miners were easy targets. It didn't take long for the private and large company miners to get hired men—gunslingers—to watch over their mines. A gunfighter could make as much as twenty dollars per day protecting a single mine. The miners found that the robbing of their minerals, mostly silver, stopped very quickly. This caused many more murders because the outlaws didn't stop looting the mines at first. It took a few gunfighters to kill a few outlaws for the word to spread around. At the rate of up to twenty dollars per day for a hired gunman, it was still cheaper than going to the courthouse to the local law enforcement to arrest these bandits.

As you can imagine, the looting of valuable silver slowed down, due to the risk of being killed, but it did not stop outlaws from committing other crimes and murders in town and on the outskirts. As robbing continued, a courthouse was constructed and security measures were set in place. A sheriff's office was built, and many residents thought the crime would settle down, but unfortunately, it didn't stop much at first. In fact, it's reported that the local sheriff's office would receive around forty-thousand dollars per year, just in bribes. This town was wild, and even the outlaws could buy their way into crime. Here's another historical account that might paint a picture of how rough Pioche was.

Sixty percent of the homicides (murders) in Nevada that were reported from 1871 to 1872 came from Pioche. Mining continued and so did the people of this violent town. The town still lives on today, with one-thousand and thirty people calling it home.

Many of the buildings can still be visited and most of them have been restored to their former glory. Museums and stores are available to shop at and hotels are there at your service. This would be a great town to visit today. Many of the mines and their equipment are still there, as well. You can really get an idea of what Pioche was like back in the 1800s. I would definitely put this town on your list if you like exploring old ghost towns, still populated or not.

When it comes to treasures and buried caches in Pioche, you need to talk with the locals. Some researchers say that the treasure to find is at the Boot Hill Cemetery. Many believe that these graves hold valuables buried with the body they belonged to. I would not suggest digging up old graves, but I can send you in a different direction. The Wells Fargo wagon was robbed many times through the years at Pioche. I would start checking into the records and people involved.

What was robbed?

Who is known or thought to have robbed it?

From there you should be able to narrow down some locations. If you need it, my other book, *Treasures of the Ancients: The Search for America's Lost Fortunes,* can help you understand local history and legends. This is a great way to find treasures that are truly lost. Another thing to think about is the price of gold and silver today. Many old mines were shut down when gold and silver prices were too low to make a profit. That's not the case today. Many private and large mining companies are thriving today. I know many prospectors that go out on the weekend to prospect for minerals and pan for gold. Some of them have made quite a lot of money from it. I would investigate it if you're living in this area. From what I've been told, you may be one of the only people on the outskirts of this once feisty town.

Now I'm going to take you to a legend that has been talked about since the beginning of the town's history: Tombstone, Arizona. This was the booming mining camp that turned into much more than that. Some of the most talked about gunfights and outlaw gangs were involved with Tombstone. Not to mention some of the most famous lawmen, too. The year 1879 is when I would like to start this story. Due to the migration of many to the west, some towns received their fair share of cattlemen, gunfighters, businessmen, outlaws, and thieves. Tombstone was a hot spot for all the above. Being so close to the border of Mexico, it acted as a safety point for outlaws to commit a crime and flee across the border.

The murder rates were higher than in our modern-day cities. After a couple more years, large deposits of silver were discovered and Tombstone became the Queen of the boomtowns in the wild west. Even though this started as a mining camp, Tombstone had all the latest fashions that many major cities had in those days. Because of its good fortune, over 100 outlaws and bandits formed a gang. Today this gang is known as the Clanton Gang, or more commonly as the "Cow Boys." There is a space between the name when you refer to the outlaws.

This was known as the first organized crime in America at the time. Murders and robberies were a way of life in Tombstone. These Cow Boys ruled the area for a very long time. The town was growing so fast that neither the marshal nor sheriff could keep up with this gang. The Cow Boys did pretty much whatever they wanted and no one was willing or able to fight back. The townspeople were outgunned and outnumbered. To this day, some people believe that the local sheriff, a man named John Harris Behan, was more of an opportunist rather than a lawman. He opened several businesses in Tombstone and made a pretty good life for himself.

Talk of temptation and bribery was whispered around town, specifically that Behan allowed the Cow Boys to run the town. Many claimed that Behan knew it was good for business and he cared more about money than stopping the outlaws. Can you imagine a large gang of outlaws coming into town? Think about the money they spent while they were there. Hotels, liquor, and women. Not to mention the gambling and supplies of goods that were purchased. Sadly, this was a fact of life, and the outlaws were helping the town prosper with cash flow from their various criminal exploits and enterprises.

By this time in history, silver mines and mine dumps could be seen all over town. Some of these mines were several miles out of town while some of them lie right underneath the town itself. There was no stopping this growth, and why would anyone do that anyway?

Modern-day Tombstone—Photo taken by author's brother, David Draper

The Cow Boys had their way with everyone until a moment, still frozen in time, changed everything. Fed White was the first town marshal of Tombstone. He was known as a friendly and good lawman. He allowed the townspeople and the Cow Boys to run their way around town unless it got out of hand. One night was far too wild for Marshal White to ignore and with the advice and support of Wyatt Earp, the marshal was about to have his hands full. During the night of October 27th, 1880, several of the Cow Boys drank and had fun for several hours in town. Marshall White heard several guns firing off in town by Allen Street.

When White entered that part of town, he found that Curly Bill Brocius was very intoxicated. Due to the fear that Curly Bill would hurt the townspeople, White approached him to disarm him. Because Curly Bill was drunk, he handed his gun to White with the barrel pointing at him. The intoxicated Curly Bill hit the trigger and that's the last thing the White heard. The gunshot ended his life. Wyatt Earp was standing by, watching the whole thing. Earp took the matter into his own hands because of his experience as a lawman himself. When Earp arrested Curly Bill, a squabble started.

The other Cow Boys ordered Earp to let Curly Bill loose. Earp refused to do so, and the townspeople were hauling in the crowd to hang Curly Bill for killing White. Earp made his own decision and took Curly Bill to jail. This was the start of a very long murder streak. The town was full of cruelty and animosity between the Cow Boys and the Earp's.

The rivalry continued, and the town was torn in two because of it. The fight at the OK Corral is one of the most famous events to happen at Tombstone. Lawmen were forsaken and outlaws were running the area, trying to stay away from Doc Holliday, Wyatt Earp, and several other appointed deputies. It didn't stop at the OK Corral; that only added fuel to the fire. That race was on and one of the opposing groups had to either kill or be killed. At the end of this story, many of the Cow Boys were killed, and the ones that weren't decided to run to save their lives. Morgan Earp was shot and killed.

Doc Holliday became sicker and eventually died of tuberculosis. He is still remembered in history as a good friend to Wyatt. He was also known as a heavy drinker and gambler. He was a dentist in his early life and his schooling earned him recognition as an educated person. Wyatt left town after the Cow Boys were pushed out and fell in love with a new woman. Later in this book, I'll get more into the individual lives of Wyatt and Doc Holliday. For now, this story is about the town. I think it's safe to say that the town of Tombstone had a very long run of mishaps and terrible situations. Outlaws still came and left the town as it moved on, continuing its silver mining process. In the modern day, Tombstone is a very popular place to visit. The town's spirit did not die along with some of the famous people from its the past.

You can visit Tombstone and see its rich history. Buildings, salons, and much more still stand today. This is a hotspot for the old west. Whether you want to see the history or hunt for lost treasures, Tombstone is still on the map and in a major way. If you're a treasure hunter, I would like to share some stories with you, and if you're not a treasure hunter, this might just change your mind.

There's a place called Skeleton Canyon, outside of Tombstone, Arizona, that is holding on to secrets of a treasure. Today it is known as the Skeleton Canyon Treasure of 1881. It's an original title and name, isn't it? Jose Estrada and his gang of bandits robbed a bank in Monterrey, Mexico. The bank had diamonds, gold bars, silver bars, and several bags of gold and silver coins. This outlaw gang took one million dollars' worth of diamonds, thirty-nine gold bars, and dozens of bags full of coins. There was even a gold statue that belonged to the church in the bank vault. That was taken as well. This was a heavy load for these outlaws to pack around and their presence did not go unnoticed.

The outlaws started heading in the southeast direction and crossed over the border of Arizona. Remember that I mentioned Curly Bill Brocius? Well, he and his gang were in the desert, ready to ambush Jose Estrada and his gang for their riches. This gunfight was combined with other unknown outlaws and cattle rustlers. According to legend, it was a double cross-type situation. Curly Bill had to know what Jose's gang was doing and where they were heading to pull off this type of fight.

Jose and his gang were shot and killed. Curly Bill's gang spread out to collect all the valuables from the bank robbery. During the fight, several mules, carrying heavy bags and riches, headed up Skeleton Canyon in the Chiricahua wilderness. Curly's gang spent a couple of days tracking down these mules and a lot of the riches were buried near Davis Mountain, by Morenci. Rumor has it that the rest of the valuables ended up at Tombstone a few days later, spent on liquor and women. Not long after this, Curly's gang of outlaws were hunted down and killed by gunshot, and the rest were hanged.

Legend says that other than some coins used in Tombstone, the outlaws didn't have time before their deaths to go and retrieve their buried treasure. The word is that there are two different sites that are holding the treasure. Still today, some people that are aware of this hidden treasure are looking for it. I've given you the mountain range and the vicinity of the buried caches. I suggest if you live in the area, go see what you can find. Find more local history and legends to learn more about it. This treasure today would be worth millions and millions of dollars.

There's an old rough town called Deadwood, tucked away in the Black Hills mountains of South Dakota. A gold strike hit this area in 1874. Many people migrated to the area soon after. Deadwood was another town that emerged from a small mining camp of canvas tents to a large town overnight. The town's highest recorded population reached a surging twenty-five thousand people strong. This would make Deadwood one of the largest cities in old western history at the time. The town got its name from miners discovering gold deposits in the mountain range and finding dead trees (timbers) surrounding the area. Quickly, the miners decided to call it Deadwood, but I think the name stuck around, not only for the dead trees but for the murders that were about to strike the town site. The law had no presence at Deadwood for some time.

Because it was claimed as an illegal town, built on Indian territory, the United States and American law could not interfere for some time. During this time, not only did people in other parts of the U.S. talk about a place of opportunity and possibilities of striking it rich, outlaws and criminals saw this lawless town as a chance to strike it rich by doing what they did best—killing and stealing for their benefit. Businessmen and entrepreneurs felt that their time had come, and many took a chance in this very fast-growing town.

Many famous people came to town. Names like James Butler Hickok, better known as Wild Bill Hickok. His name preceded him as a soldier, scout, lawman, and famous gunfighter. He was involved with many known shootouts before he arrived at Deadwood. This was a man who was respected but feared by many, all at the same time. This town was so wild that Wild Bill Hickok was shot and killed after only being there a few short weeks. August 2, 1876, was the date of his murder. He was gambling at the Nuttal & Mann's Saloon. A man named Jack McCall shot him while Bill was playing poker. This wasn't a clean kill. Bill was shot from behind, ending his life. It's said that Bill was holding a pair of aces and eights in his hand when he was shot. Jack claimed that he killed Wild Bill Hickok to avenge his brother's death in Deadwood.

Jack McCall had a nickname of "Crooked Nose" and would have possibly gone through life unrecognized by history if he hadn't killed Wild Bill Hickok. After the shooting, he was arrested and tried for the murder, but it wouldn't hold up in court because the crime was committed on native land. During this time, he was taken to McDaniel's Theater and was found not guilty of his crime. He was set free and later, while he was in Wyoming, he spent some time bragging about how he murdered Wild Bill and that's how he ended up in the court system. He was then taken to Yankton, retried, and found guilty. Jack was hung until dead.

Later, this saloon was nicknamed "Dead Man's Hand." Bill was placed in the World Series of Poker's Hall of Fame and his name has been known by history and many folklore storytellers. This was only the start of this lawless town. Many of the good people in town had to act as lawmen by taking on the task of weeding out the good from the bad. It wasn't unusual for the townspeople to decide and determine who was guilty and who was not.

Many hangings took place in this town without law enforcement and a courthouse. This was truly a place that was in the hands of those who lived there and what they thought was right. There was no judge to listen to the pleas of the accused. If the townspeople decided someone was guilty or not guilty, that's the way it was.

Deadwood was talked about in conversations all around the United States. Others came through this town to see and take in the culture and lifestyle for a short time. People like Wyatt Earp, Theodore Roosevelt, and even Babe Ruth visited it at times. Due to the activities and people, this town has many lost treasures to be found. Not only is the history rich—along with the Black Hills gold mines—but this town also presented many opportunities for outlaws.

I'll give you a couple of stories about lost treasure in the area so you can see that there are still possibilities for new discoveries, but it'll somewhat more explain the history of the town. In 1879, two prospectors named Humphrey and Shafer had a mining claim where they also built a small cabin. This mining claim was on the west side of Bear Mountain just about ten miles from Hill City. The two prospectors struck it rich with gold and decided to bury around one million dollars of gold nuggets close to the cabin for safekeeping. At this time, the nearby towns didn't have a bank and the area was too wild to trust anyone else with their fortune, so they kept the gold out of sight so no one could find it.

Like many old western towns, secrets didn't stay hidden for very long. A few outlaws heard the story of gold nuggets buried by their cabin and they decided to pursue it. The outlaws found the cabin and the prospectors, tied them up, and questioned them about where the gold was hidden. Humphrey and Shafer would not tell the outlaws the exact location, even when they were faced with death. After some time, the outlaws grew tired and frustrated with the prospectors and they murdered them without ever finding the gold. Legend says that the gold was never found and that it's still there, by the old cabin, waiting to be discovered.

There's another story of a payroll robbery around Deadwood. Apparently, some outlaws robbed a payroll that was meant for the working fees of the miners of the Holy Terror Mine. These outlaws took the caches of around thirty thousand dollars of gold and silver coins, then went into the town of Deadwood. The outlaws are mentioned in history for using gold and silver coins in town for services like hotel rooms, a bath, and drinking at the saloon, but the men were never approached by anyone for the robbery. Rumors from the townspeople are that the outlaws only had a few coins each while they were seen in town. A short few days into their gambling and drinking, they were shot and killed.

Deadwood, South Dakota—1876

It's said that the hotel never found the rest of the payroll coins after clearing their rooms and belongings. Many think the outlaws buried most of the coins just outside of town. I believe the history of Deadwood is enough for me, but if others want to search for other types of riches from the past, I know that Deadwood would be a great place to look. Even though I can go on and on about Deadwood town, I'm going to press forward and tell you about a few more wild towns of the old west.

Let's move on to a city that has been known to history for a very long time: Santa Fe, New Mexico. Now this story is quite a bit different than the towns that I mentioned earlier in the chapter. When you think of open ranges and old western movies of desperados and cattlemen fighting for their lands, this is one of those places that comes to mind. This area was claimed and unclaimed by so many that it's hard to know who really owned it. I'm going to take you further back in time so you can see the difference in this area when it comes to old western history. Santa Fe vicinity was claimed by the famous conquistador Francisco Vasquez de Coronado in 1540. It would soon become a stronghold of Spain for religion and faith. During this time, the Spanish converted over one hundred thousand Pueblo Indians to their Catholic ways.

Three Pueblo Indian Woman Selling Baskets in the New Mexico Territory

Times did change, though, and in 1680, the Pueblo Indians rebelled against the Spanish, killing around 400 of them. Out of fear for their lives, the Spanish moved south back to Mexico. The Indians then destroyed most of the Spanish buildings and reclaimed the area. This was typical for Indians to do. They wanted to erase the bad and move on with their lives. Spain didn't give up on Santa Fe very easily, and from this point, events continued to happen. The Spanish spent the next few years attacking the Indians from different points and locations. Many small villages were attacked and the Spanish did everything they could to break the spirits of the Indians.

From this point on, Santa Fe had a lot of cultural behavior changes. The battle of the local Indians continued on for many more years, and Spain tried to reclaim the area once again. Many cattlemen and farmers also tried to rebel against any Mexican rule that existed throughout the area. Then later the Mexican War happened between 1846 and 1848. This event led to the area becoming annexed as part of the United States.

New Mexico and Santa Fe were changing with the times. Later on, a few more years later, this town was used during the Civil War by General Henry Dibley. He stayed in the area for only around a month but he did fly the Confederate flag while he was there with his troops. Not long after that, the Santa Fe Railroad changed much of Santa Fe's economy but not everyone wanted this area to change with time. This is when Santa Fe became a wild west town, even though it already had its share of history before that. Even Billy the kid was said to have threatened to kill Governor Lew Wallace because of the changes he made in the territory.

By 1912, the population of Santa Fe was around five thousand residents and from here it started to change as many other towns did. Even today, the town is considered small and many of the people that live there are connected to the history by several generations.

When I think of New Mexico, I think of a good John Wayne movie showing how this place was free and wild. A landowner with the strength to keep others from claiming their land lived a very interesting and busy life. Mexicans and outlaws came into the area to hide from the law and took advantage of the wide-open spaces. Some of the neighboring cattlemen had problems with cattle thieves, sometimes from the landowners of the area themselves. Billy the Kid worked and lived in and out of this area as well.

Today, many people come from all over the place and stop to visit Santa Fe. It's still on the old Route 66 and that helps bring in people looking to get a taste of history. There's plenty to see there and many old buildings downtown. Even new construction consists of old-type designs that keep Santa Fe locked in the old days. If you're looking for treasures, all you must do is do some research and you'll find many stories of lost and buried treasures around this town. From what I've investigated, I think there's still plenty in the area to go after. If you're someone that believes the treasure is the history instead of the gold and silver, you'll find that at Santa Fe too.

Now I would like to move on to a place that is full of outlaw history and it'll take us to the northeast, this palace is named Dodge City of Kansas. Dodge City may not be what everyone thought and heard; it was a very bad and dangerous town. The truth is between 1873 and 1875, there were no reported murders or violent crimes committed in Dodge City, but that wasn't always the case. Let's go into the early history of 1872. Dodge City was founded and discovered by 12 men pioneers while the Santa Fe Railroad laid tracks down in the area. Soon after these men set up camp and started the town, it became a shipping center location from the trail to sell and store supplies and goods that shipped east to west. Because of the railroad, it attracted small business owners and cattle ranchers to the area.

Buffalo hides from hunters were coming to town fast and that started a new line of work as well. Many people travel on the trails from Texas and other states, and Dodge City became a place to buy and sell livestock and this attracted outlaws and bandits. During this time, residents and businessmen of Dodge City wanted to spread the word that Dodge City was coming up and the town was thriving. They hoped by giving information to newspapers around the United States, the town would continue to grow. Business owners invested their hard-earned money into the town, and a larger population would mean more money.

Unfortunately, some newspapers embellished the truth, stretched it out some would say. In fact, many newspapers were just flat-out lying about how many murders were taking place. The town was lawless, and some murders were committed, but not to the point of the place being worse off than other towns. Because of news spreading that Dodge City was out of control, it seemed to attract more outlaws than good people. The town suffered for a couple more years when it came to its economics. Outlaws came into town, looking for the next robbery, and crime was still above average for a town of its size.

Main Street of Dodge City, Kansas—1878

There was no law or courthouse, and the state of Kansas started working on a solution to help the townspeople.

A death toll report showed that eighteen murders had been committed in Dodge City throughout its time. Once the state of Kansas received word of that, they took action by approving law and order in the town and providing the finances to do that. Another two years went by before a marshal arrived, and that was the start of the town gaining back control. The first marshal tried his best to be a deterrent, but some days were harder than others. Outlaws still had their gunfights and outbursts that disturbed the normal way of life and it took someone else to really change the way Dodge City was.

Wyatt Earp already had a reputation as a lawman, and he was known for his demeanor and grit. He was appointed the law after handling a shootout with confidence. This is really where he earned his place and was known to not take any guff from anyone. The law was passed and enforced that no one can carry a gun into town. Everyone was able to practice open carry, but not within the town limits. If you came into town with a gun, you had to check it in at the county jail.

Earp was fighting the crime by not allowing guns to be used as weapons. This did slow down gunfights, robberies, and drunken accidents. Earp didn't do it alone, though. He had several men sworn in to help him. That included his older brother, Virgil Earp, and his younger brother, Morgan Earp. Bat Masterson was among Earp's deputies, as well. They were ready to make a difference. This wasn't easy for many outlaws to take in, essentially the Clements gang. Wyatt Earp and his lawmen stopped the Clements gang in the middle of the street one night as he was holding a shotgun, and pointed right at them. The gang was riding their horses in town with guns blazing. The law was waiting for them. This is where the real stand happened between good and evil. After some words, the gang backed down and checked their guns. A law was also passed banning public intoxication.

As you can imagine, the town's jailhouse was quite full most of the time. Earp was fair, and once the person sobered up, they were released. News and stories started to spread and after a long battle of enforcing what seemed to be unheard of laws, the lawmen did prevail. The town of Dodge City had law and order. Later, Wyatt and his group moved on to Tombstone, Arizona, to get away from the law work and to start their own business. When it comes to lost treasures around Dodge City, I've tracked down information that mentions a Wells Fargo stagecoach that was robbed. Just west of the town, a group of outlaws attacked and robbed a Wells Fargo wagon and stole its contents.

The gold and silver coins, including paper dollars, were never found. Many people think this buried treasure is still outside of the town limits. Good old stories of these disappearing towns have always intrigued me, and I've spent a lot of my life exploring these places along with looking for any hidden treasures along the way. Sadly, many of these old towns are no longer standing. Some of these old towns have burnt down to the ground. Some of them have decayed away with time, and some have been torn down by modern-day activities. The touristy old towns are great for seeing scripted gunfight shows and getting into the history of what events made the town famous. The towns I mentioned above are those types of towns and I highly suggest visiting them.

You will have lots of great memories if you visit them. For some of you that really like to see some old buildings that are not in a state park, you will have to travel off the route a little. They are still out there; I've seen them with my own two eyes. I can't explain the wonders that come withstanding at an old town site, knowing the history behind it. Many times, I've taken a step back and looked at the old buildings, imagining what they may have looked like in their wildest times. These old towns that are not protected and made into national parks are almost all gone now. I don't think they are going to last much longer. In the last twenty years, I've seen what I called "good conditioned" old ghost towns and revisited them eight years later to see that buildings and structures are on their last legs.

If you have the opportunity to visit some of these old ghost towns, don't hesitate. You may not get another chance. I'm going to list a few old towns below in the hopes that some of you will go visit them and see what I mean. Please respect the buildings and the landowners if anyone owns them. Take pictures while you are out there. I'm guessing within twenty more years, ninety percent of them will be destroyed. Also remember, if you're a treasure hunter or historical researcher, a burnt downtown with no buildings doesn't mean everything is gone. A little bit of research and some metal detectors can allow you to pull lost history out of the ground. It may be artifacts that haven't been seen for over a hundred years or more. Some of these towns are more off the beaten trail than others.

Some still have residents that are watching over the sites and some are modern-day towns with original buildings. If you check the history of your state, I know you can find some abandoned places and ghost towns within a few hours of your home.

Silver City, Idaho—Photo taken by David Draper

- Silver City, Idaho
- St Elmo, Colorado
- Terlingua, Texas
- Bodie, California
- Nelson, Nevada
- Virginia City, Montana
- Custer, Idaho
- Bannack, Montana
- South Pass City, Wyoming
- Kennecott, Alaska
- Goldfield, Arizona
- Nevada City, Montana
- Rhyolite, Nevada
- Frisco, Utah
- Madrid, New Mexico

If you're looking for a few ghost towns to visit that have the old feeling but are more accommodating, like tourist attractions, here's a list below. Most of them are on the main route, easy to drive to, and have many events to make your visit enjoyable.

- Telluride, Colorado
- Deadwood, South Dakota
- Dodge City, Kansas
- Tombstone, Arizona
- Calico, California
- Bodie, California

THREE

Mining Camps and Settlements

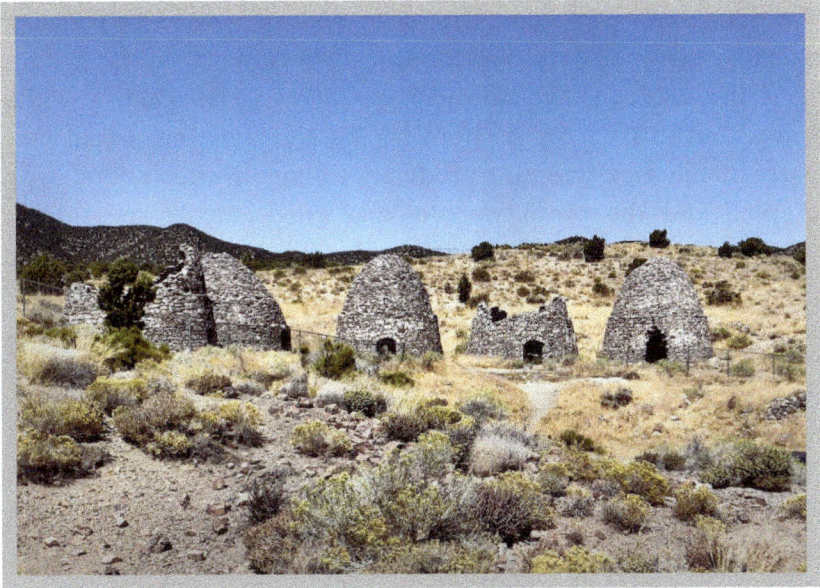

Kilns at Frisco, Utah mining town

What is a mining camp? This word has been used for around two hundred years in the U.S. but what's the real meaning of the word?

It's true that the word mining camp has been loosely used for a very long time now, referring to any camp that is used for mining. Big. Small. It's a mining camp. Back during the gold rush era, many mining camps set up canvas tents for a mess hall, doctors' offices, saloons, and just about anything that needed a roof. It was not practical for miners to find a little flash in their pans and just start building a town. Some minerals and veins would only last a few weeks, months, and years until no more minerals were found in the area.

Many mining companies would set up shop just like a poor miner would. First, you find a source of minerals (gold, silver, iron, platinum, etc.) and from there, you would try to determine how rich the area is. Assay testing has been around for a long time, but to put it simply, old-time miners could tell by panning for gold. If their gold pan was full of gold after running a few pans through the water, they would know how many pieces of gold and make a decision from there. If the area had more than fifteen pieces of gold in the pan, that would be just enough to keep trying.

If the area was worth sticking around, small camps would spread out in the area as more testing and scouting would take place. If the area was still producing minerals after a long span of time and the profit was looking good, then some lumber would be sent to the area to build a few buildings. The first few buildings usually were assay buildings, warehouses for supplies, goods for the miners, and possibly the mine boss. These first buildings are not the kind that you see today in western movies. These were very quickly built buildings. Most of them were torn down quickly. Think of them as temporary buildings.

Now let's say that many more mineral deposits were discovered in the area and more miners and mining companies came into the area to work, then it would start the chain of progress. This progress was of businesses and supply men. The more people that came to the area and started making and producing money, the more buildings would go up. Hotels, restaurants, banks, saloons, stores, and much more. If there was a temporary building in the way of construction, these cheaply made buildings would be destroyed and new, better-built buildings would emerge.

This was practical and many mining camps started off this way. Not all mining camps became large cities. Some of them stayed small and grew over a long period of time. Some mining camps within a year of finding minerals would have a population of over three thousand residents. Some mining camps were nothing more than a tent city but the miners stayed and mined for over ten years. It was all about the money and opportunities.

If it made sense, then they welcomed growth. Now that I explained that a little bit, I want you to consider how many mining camps and towns were set up and built from the mid-eighteen hundreds to the early nineteen hundreds.

The beginnings of a mining camp in the 19th Century

I'll save you time: thousands and thousands. You don't hear about that part, do you? Many old western towns are frequently mentioned. Many of them I spoke of in the last chapter. Did a big town and fancy name define the success of the gold and silver that came out of the area? That depends on who you talk to. Some people believed that a big mining company meant success and someone different. Here's something to think about. I've been told so many stories that have been passed down about a small group or sometimes one man that kept a secret so well that no one knew about it. If the miner was smart and distant enough from an established town, he would sometimes mine that area for his whole life. Don't doubt it.

It happened more than once and in more than one place, I can guarantee you that. It's important for you to know this because, one, it's part of our American history and culture, and two, there may be old mining camps in the mountains that modern explorers have not yet discovered. Or maybe someone has but didn't know what they stumbled upon. Today these old mining camps wouldn't look like mining camps. It would look like disturbed ground, possibly with old rusty iron artifacts on the ground. It's possible that most of the camp is now concealed by vegetation and dirt.

These mining camps were one hundred percent lawless. If the camp was full of bad people that had intentions of hurting and robbing people, there wasn't much that could be done to stop them. The only good people possibly were retired lawmen, gunmen, retired military, or just a brave soul. Back in those days, only the strong would survive. In all reality, there was a larger population that had good intentions towards others. The evil and cruelty were a much smaller amount but the bad always preys on the good. They take advantage of the working class people, trying to just get by.

That was many of the outlaws back in the old days. I do just have to mention another thing since I have you on this discussion. Even people that do bad things can be good people. Some of these outlaws didn't know any better, and good people sometimes got in the way. Not every outlaw was a brutal killer. Because these mining camps were helpless against outlaws, many robberies and stolen goods were a regular event. If a group of outlaws spotted a mining camp in the hills and saw that only eight men were in camp, there was a good chance that the camp was staked and later attacked.

If some of the miners were still alive after the robbery, they would ride into the closest town with the law and give a description of the outlaws. Many outlaws and bandits were chased down by posses. Some of the outlaws would bury or hide the stolen goods and flee that area. Some of these outlaws were caught by the posses and were shot and killed during a gunfight. Some were arrested and taken back to town and were hanged.

This is a lot of information and description because I want you to see and picture what life was like back in the old days. I want you to see the possibilities of lost history and treasures. Not to mention that mines that are still in these areas are possibly undiscovered.

I see mystery and adventure when I think of mining camps. They could be some of the last untouched places by man since the mining era. The tourist attraction towns are fun and great but I guarantee that everyone has gone through these places. Visitors have checked the sideways and up and down. The small and forgotten mining camps are just as I call them, lost. I have found many, many old mining areas in my time. I'm always on the lookout for more. Learning about the history, what was mined in the area, and which outlaws were involved, now that sounds like a good lesson to have.

I will give you a hint on how to find these old sites. In 1872, the mining law was set in place for all Americans. One thing that every miner had to do was stake a claim and file their paperwork. To stake their claim, it was simple. All they had to do was build three-foot monuments made of wood or stone and place them at the four corners of their mining claim. Then they would have to go and file their claim location, their name, and what minerals they discovered. A small fee was paid, and then they were done. Off to mining they would go. Now these days, the county offices should still have old records of the mining claims that were filed.

I've been to many city buildings, going through large books that had thousands of mining claim paperwork in them. Another great thing is that many county and state offices are making digital copies of these documents. Depending on what state you live in, you can simply go online and start searching for old mining claim papers. If you can find some, now you have the location and some names that were involved. From there, I would reach out and find historians and scholars of the area. If families have lived in the area for many generations, reach out to them. They might have a good story to tell.

Now that you have that information, you can become an explorer of the old wild west, tracking down lost history and mines. You can learn much about the outlaws in your state and look for their lost history as well. Discovering western history is still one of my favorite things to do. If you do go out and explore, be careful of your surroundings. I promise you that it can make a difference and you might find a great treasure. Whether it be lost information, an adventure, or something worth value.

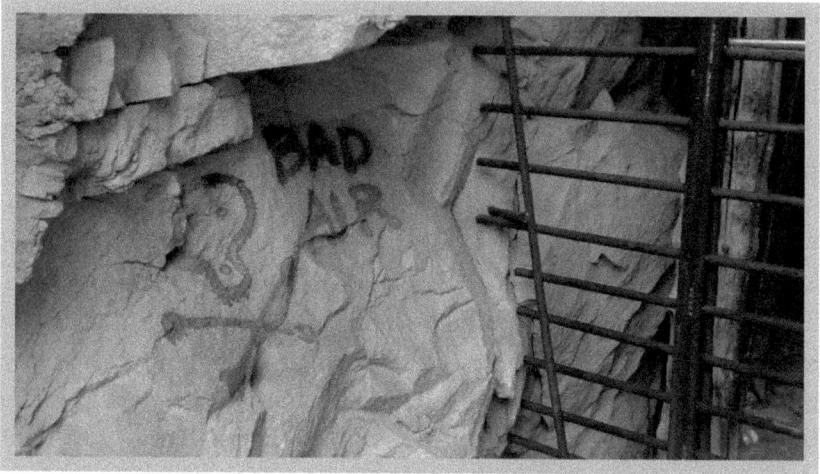

Bad Air: A barred up mine entrance and a sign of danger

FOUR

Marks that the Outlaws Targeted

Before we get into what drove the outlaws' crime, let's go a little into their backstory. This way we can understand their behaviors and what makes them tick. After the Civil War, many Confederates were still hung up on what they lost from the war and what they didn't gain. Depending on what person you hear the story from, some would say the Confederate soldiers were the guys that turned outlaws. In fact, history shows that in many stories. Just remember, many Confederates lost their land, homes, and much more during the war. I guess it would be safe to say that some of them were bitter and angry.

Some of them wanted to ignite the war again with hate and discontent. That being said, there were a lot of Confederate soldiers that also did well for our county. Wyatt Earp was a confederate and he was one of them that helped change things for the better. It's also safe to say that not all outlaws were Confederates either. Some outlaws were just people that did wrong things due to lifestyle, childhoods, and other situations that could be explained in a way that they just didn't know any better. Just like in today's world, there are many criminals in the world but not all of them would commit rape, hurt a child, or even murder someone.

Some of these outlaws were cowards and their names would have never been remembered except for their last decision to shoot a man from behind. What I'm trying to say is, that different things drove different men to the life of crime. Let's not forget that outlaws were not just male figures. There were ruthless females known in history for being outlaws, too. I'll go more into that later in this book. Let's look at some of the outlaws that came from the south. Some of these outlaws came back from the war to find that they lost everything.

Some came home to find that their home was nothing but ashes, smoldering in the dirt. Others arrived in their hometown, only to find that their family was murdered. Some of these outlaws didn't have a family and they were out for revenge against the whole world. Some of them suffered from mental illnesses and situations that robbed them of the good things in life. I think there were many reasons for outlaws to do what they did. Another thing to consider is that the old west was much different than it is now. In many ways, being the nice guy would not get you ahead in that time. In fact, it could have ended your life. You had to be rough and tough.

If your parents were born in the 1940s and earlier, you know what I mean. Our parents and their parents were tough people. Hard working and ready to take on whatever came before them. This mentality came from the old days and was passed down to their children. Now, let's get to some of the exciting parts of the old west. The west was growing very fast and many establishments were sitting ducks when it came to bad men coming into the territory. The land was up for the taking, and I'm not just talking about the famous land grab either. Some of the best gunfighters fought for the land of their own and once they got it many had to continue fighting to keep it theirs. As towns and development grew, more and more supply trains started heading west, full of many valuables. Jesse James and his gang are a great example.

They would create roadblocks on the tracks and force the engineer to stop the train in an emergency situation in a hurry. Once the train stopped, the helpless, unarmed passengers were robbed of all the goods and anything valuable, and the vaults and safes on the trains were blown to smithereens. Jesse James committed many robberies, and he wasn't the only outlaw that had a gang robbing trains. Bill Downing, Bill Miner, and Elmer McCurdy were other outlaws that robbed trains as well. They all wanted the same thing, to steal and get anything of value to better their finances.

Train along the Old Spanish Trail

Here's the thing, many outlaws had their class of what they robbed. It wasn't all just train and bank robberies. Stagecoaches and miners were targeted, too. The famed outlaws that you mostly hear about in history are usually the ones that pulled off the big heists. The train and bank robberies were a small percentage of the robberies. These make good stories to tell but the smaller crimes that took place were a much larger percentage of the frequent outlaw crimes. For instance, Jesse James and his group robbed about twenty trains in the span of their criminal lives. An outlaw named Milton Sharp was known for robbing stagecoaches and he robbed over twenty in his time. Stagecoach robberies outnumbered train robberies twenty to one. That's a big difference.

The risk of a successful miner getting robbed for his few gold nuggets was an even higher percentage than stagecoaches. See where I'm going with this? History tells about the big stories but very little was written about someone. Even fewer stories are told today about the smaller crimes. The way it goes today, if Hollywood doesn't make an old western movie about it, it didn't happen. If an author doesn't do his or her research or broadens their writing, the story can be lost forever. I've spent most of my adult life researching and hunting after lost history and treasures. Sometimes the treasure consists of lost artifacts or some riches but most of the time, it's the lost information and evidence that I find in the field.

In my book *Treasures of the Ancients: The Search for America's Lost Fortunes*, I save the best part of the book for last. At the end, I share with the reader many different lost treasure sites and historical evidence that can point someone in the right direction to finding new history. I list over two hundred treasure locations and I include treasure stories in every state of the United States. This book would be very enlightening to you because you will see that many of these lost treasure sites have to do with events taking place in the old west. From pirate treasures to outlaw treasures, you will see that many of them are from the civil war to the end of the old west in the early twentieth century.

So, let's go into some of the less known stories of outlaws. We'll focus on the big and well-known stories later. Depending on the outlaw, some people were robbed just walking out of town from the saloon at night. Some outlaws would hurt innocent people just for the few silver coins they have in their pockets. Another vicious crime that took place in the old days was outlaws tailing a wagon trail of families while traveling on a well-known trail. This was a very common occurrence that took place on the Oregon Trail. So many unmarked graves were dug along this trail. These smaller wagon trains were easy targets for outlaws.

Some of these families were traveling with money and other valuables that would prove to be a good payday for some. It was common for these outlaws to follow wagon trains from afar to study the group. After a few days of staying back and observing the group, the outlaws could see if the men had guns and what type of possessions they had in their wagons. When the time was right, they would attack. Early morning or nighttime was the best. If the outlaws attacked in the early morning when most of the group was still sleeping, they would have a better chance of attacking successfully.

The same goes for nighttime squabbles. Now some of the outlaws had more morals than others. Some outlaws would capture the group's people, tie them up, and rob their things without people getting shot or worse, killed. What bad and heartless outlaws, you know where I'm going and why there are so many burial sites and tombstones on these old trails. In some events, the outlaws had no choice. If a person tried to protect themselves, family members, and/or belongings, a flight could have broken loose, and someone could have been shot stabbed with a knife. This happened fairly often because this was the old west. Nothing was simple and easy going back then.

This goes the same with many crimes that were committed. The outlaws didn't always have the intent to kill. In fact, many of them wanted money, gold, silver, or whatever was of value but didn't want to kill others. That's why these old western stories are so famous. Unfortunately, when a tragedy happened and people were killed, the story or crime was remembered. Many news companies in the 1800s would embellish stories of crime so more people would read their newspapers. This is similar to what happens in modern-day media as well. Who likes a doll, a boring story? No one. Because of the exaggerations, many of the historical stories can only be taken to heart so much.

The sad thing is if a crime or murder was committed with no names of public figures, or unknown outlaws, the stories would go untold. Another crime that happened a lot was a massacre. Now many massacres were written about if many people were involved and murdered. Unfortunately, these types of heinous crimes happened a lot more than many of us want to admit. Many native Indians were slaughtered this way, and the door swung the other way as well, where Indians killed white people, too. This is a horrible circle of life in the old days. The Native Indians wanted the white people off their land and the white people wanted the natives to go away.

More than once, I've learned that our U.S. government and military troops used politics to justify what happened to so many Indian tribes. Many of these massacres happened and if Natives were killed, the white man was set free and clear of their crimes. The outlaws used this to their advantage. If they were ever caught murdering others, often they blamed it on local natives.

Some of the outlaws would go as far as dressing like Indians and even leaving arrows in their victim's bodies to point the cavalry to a local tribe for the murders. Native Indians had a bad reputation so it was not hard to convince the judge or jury of that. I'm sure you can see where this caused more confusion and vexation between American citizens and the native Indians that had claims on the land much earlier than any foreigner that migrated to the new world. Now let's go into what outlaws are targeted and why. Banks are an obvious choice. Not just for paper dollar bills, but for those that are stored in a bank. An outlaw would find the bank's vaults and safety deposit boxes full of gold and silver coins, jewelry, and gold and silver bars.

Not to mention that many banks were holding places for gold and silver ore and bars from nearby mining companies. Banks were not as heavily guarded as you would think. Depending on the size of the town, some banks had no protection at all. I've run across many stories where the outlaws were able to make a clean get-a-way and the only people that tried to stop them were townspeople. No law. No security. That risk was always present for outlaws in the wild west days. Many people carried guns and weren't afraid to use them if necessary. Most bank robberies hurt the people of the town. The type of insurance that's in place now, is not what people had in the old days.

If someone robbed a bank, everyone in the town lost their money and valuables. It was common for people to fight back. Many posses that were formed were done with normal, everyday people that wanted to bring the outlaws back to pay for their crimes. Banks were robbed less often than a stagecoach. Now that stagecoaches were a big and easier target. Some of the high dollar, heavily loaded stagecoaches had many armed men to protect their content but that was not enough in some cases. Picture this. A stagecoach is moving along a canyon with a driver, a man riding shotgun, and six other men on horses. All of them would be armed with long range rifles and six-shooters for short range. These men would do their best to keep a close out of trouble, but many outlaws were experienced and smart with their plans.

A canyon would make it easy to set up an ambush. The outlaws could stay hidden behind brush and rocks to stay out of sight. They could wait for the stagecoach to get in the right area and start to shoot before anyone would know what was happening. Even when the guns started firing, many times the protectors of the stagecoach were sitting ducks and out in the open. Many robberies happened like this. A rich stagecoach was easy to find and follow because the richer the cargo was, the more men would be protecting it. Sometimes that law wouldn't know for days that a stagecoach was attacked. Stagecoaches were delayed all the time from weather and other mishaps. Sometimes, by the time it was known that a stagecoach was robbed, the outlaws had already had plenty of time to escape.

This made it more likely that these outlaw gangs would continue with their robberies in the future. If you can get away with it the first time, why not try it again, and again? Don't forget about how many people meet their match on trails, in the saloons, or at their mining claims. The outlaws would literally rob and steal whatever they thought would help their pockets grow bigger. Now going back to Confederate outlaws after the war, some of these robberies and attacks were more thought out. Some of the heists were planned by the outlaws before the attack and it wasn't always about money for their pockets.

Some were to weaken the union and the government. If many planned robberies led to taking money away from the government, military, and more, some outlaws did this out of spite. It's a war technique that has been around for a very long time. If you want to hurt and weaken your opponent, take away their water and food supply, and means of transportation and funds. This continued for many years after the war. Some of the Confederate outlaws wanted the Union to suffer just like they did, even after the war. Take Billy the Kid for example. He was an outlaw and did many bad things in his life but towards the end, he felt that he was avenging his deceased employer.

Billy the Kid spent a lot of his time going after the men he felt were responsible for murdering John Tunstall. Billy believed that John was a good man that had helped him try to escape from the life of bad doing. Even though some people knew what Billy was doing was wrong and not the right way to handle these types of crimes, Billy did what he knew best dealing with people on the other side of a gun. Many townspeople wanted to arrest the people involved with John's murder, but Billy wasn't ready or willing to let it happen in court. I'll explain and go much more into Billy the Kid's life later in this book. For now, I just want you to know that not all outlaw stories are cut and dry. Or even black or white.

Let's not forget about the cattle rustlers. These types of gangs may have done better for themselves than you would think. Let's say that the common price for a cow was eighteen dollars in the 1850s, and a hard stole three hundred, that would come out to five thousand and four hundred dollars. To put that in perspective, $5,400.00 dollars would be worth around $195,000.00 dollars in today's value. Cattle was a big business back in the old days. Still today. Outlaws could make a big profit by taking cattle and driving them to the nearest town to sell the beef.

The bottom line is, that if the outlaw prospered in greed for money or determination for revenge, it happened in the old days and nothing could stop it from happening. Only death or a change of heart would stop it. It was the vicious circle of life and grit back in those days. The most unfortunate thing was that many good people got in the way of what some would call progress and some would call it a tragedy.

FIVE

Notorious Gangs of the 19th and 20th Century

I'm going to list some of the known and less known outlaw gangs below. I can't list all of them, as there were too many from this time period. Below you will find outlaws from many different parts of the old western states. Some of them were ruthless murderers and some of them were more civilized. You will find that some of them cattle rustled and some of them robbed trains. I won't go much into detail because many of these gangs will be mentioned later in this book.

This chapter will give you a better idea of what the outlaws did during their time and what was robbed. Some of these outlaws rode off into the sunset and were never heard from again. Many of them spent their days drinking and robbing. Some of these outlaws went down in history as famous people of the old west and some of them are remembered as terrible people that got what they deserved. The fact of the matter is that everyone likes a good outlaw story. It's been that way since these stories were told after they happened.

The Bummers Gang—Colorado Territory (1855-1860)

I would really like to start with a gang that I find interesting, not only for their name but for living up to it. The Bummers Gang was full of bums, just like the name suggests. This wasn't your typical gang; it was full of unemployed and lazy bandits that didn't amount to a whole lot but minor crimes. The leader's name was Eddie "the Shooter" Coleman. History and legends talk about the gang being intoxicated frequently. The crimes they committed were during the night and it became almost a nightly thing. Robbing townspeople so the gang can get drunk the next day. The townspeople of Auraria Colorado grew tired of their crimes and the local sheriff formed a posse to chase down each gang member.

The posse ended up arresting a few of them at the same time, and those men had a trial in court which led to them hanging on the gallows. Once these outlaws were dead, the sheriff continued his hunt to find every single one of the gang members. Over a course of time, all of them were arrested and hanged.

Lincoln County Regulators—New Mexico Territory (1878-1878)

This was the famous gang that Billy the Kid, Doc Scurlock, and Jose Chavez started in the New Mexico territory and was later called the Lincoln County War. This was the war of outlaws and corporate American store owners. Billy the Kid accused the store owner Murphy of sending his hired men to track down William (John) Tunstall and kill him. Murphy was known to be a hard headed businessman that came into the area to take over town and business, using his money.

Billy the Kid admired John Tunstall because he was a likable man that made a habit of hiring outlaws to help them reform their lives.

John helped Billy learn how to read and taught him to rethink his criminal life. When John was found dead, with bullet holes in his body, Billy knew it was Murphy who ordered the murder. From that point on, John Chisum and his friends urged Bill to fight in court, not with a gun. Billy and his Regulars were not about to stand down. Murphy groups together his hired guns and townspeople call them the Murphy Gang. In the year 1878, 21 men were killed over the dispute. This story has been told for many years and this is where Billy the Kid earned his reputation.

The Wild Bunch—Colorado, Wyoming, Montana, Idaho, Nevada, and Utah Territory (1892-1895)

I'm sure you heard about Butch Cassidy and the Sundance Kid. This group was wild and they did everything from killing to drinking at the saloon. Butch Cassidy was the main leader and he was known as a good outlaw. Its' said today that Butch never killed anyone, even during all the crimes that were committed. Now many of his gang members were some of the roughest and they had no problem with murdering if need be. The Wild Bunch spent a lot of their time on the run. Even though they were known to make an appearance in familiar places from time to time, they went from town to town. Hideout to hide out.

This gang committed many robberies. Trains, payrolls, and banks. It didn't matter what the job was, if there was money to take, the Wild Butch was there. This gang was very smart and they really planned out their crimes. Using horses like a relay race to outrun the law. Most of the western states encountered the gang at some point. Many of their robberies are well known like the Castle Gate Robbery and the Wild West Railroad Crime. I'm going to share a lot more about Butch Cassidy and the Wild Bunch later in this book.

The Rio Grande Posse, aka The John Kinney Gang—New Mexico Territory (1870s-Unknown)

This gang were successful cattle rustlers part time and hired guns men the other part. Most of their work was done in the Dona Ana County area. Make no mistake, this gang also committed robberies as well. John Kinney was the lead and the one that organized the gang. They were also a part of the Murphy Gang that led to the Lincoln County War against Billy the Kid and the Regulators. These were rough men for sure. The gang members that lived during the battle of Billy the Kid, went back to Dona Ana County to continue their cattle rustling.

Some of the gang moved on at a later time and joined another group of outlaws called the Selman's Scouts and some joined the Jesse Evans Gang. Some of the gang members were not mentioned in history again but we know that John Kinney was later arrested for his gang's crime and spent three years in prison. Kenny never returned to the life of an outlaw and he joined the U.S. Army.

Black Hills Bandits—Deadwood, South Dakota Territory (1876-1877)

This was the known gang of outlaws that ruled the town of Deadwood for a short amount of time. Sam Bass, Joel Collins, Jack Davis, Tom Nixon, and a few more were the men that not only organized the gang, but they also committed the crimes. History and legends tell of the gang robbing the Deadwood Stage, stagecoach services for goods, and more. According to the story, the Black Hills Bandits robbed the stagecoach for the fifth time on March 25th, 1877. The gunshots shared the horses away from the battle and the bandits found themselves only two miles away from town.

That was their last robbery in the Deadwood area and sometime after, the gang decided to change their style of train robbing. Their first train robbery took place in Big Springs Nebraska with a disappointing four hundred and fifty dollars in one of the trains cars. They didn't give up their hunt and continued to search the cars. At one point, they discovered a few wooden boxes and broke them open to find that their heist had paid off. They took the sixty thousand dollars' worth of twenty-dollar gold coins. After the getaway, all the gang was killed except one, Sam Bass returned to his home in Round Rock Texas, and formed a new gang called the Sam Bass Gang.

The Mccanles Gang, aka Mccandless Gang—Nebraska Territory (Early 1860s)

This gang came as rough as it gets. They were known to be murderers, horse thieves, cattle rustlers, bank robbers, and trains. They did it all. David McCanles was the leader of the gang and he was known to be a bully in his hometown. He ran the gang the same way and the word ruthless was a nice thing to say about this gang. On July 12th, 1861, the McCanles gang ran into Wild Bill Hickok, and he made a name for himself by single handedly killing ten gang members that day.

Some say that when it comes to famous gunslingers like Wild Bill Hickok, the stories were often exaggerated. Some say Bill only killed three outlaws of the gang that day. Because the newspapers were known to embellish the truth, the story of what happened to the outlaw and the stolen loot is unknown today. It would take a local historian to decipher the information to learn more.

The Innocents Gang—Montana Territory (1860s)

Henry Plummer was a lawman turned outlaw. He's the one that organized the gang, and they are notorious for robbing the shipments of gold and silver that were on stagecoaches from Bannack City to Virginia City. This gang was known to stake out the road that led out of town and during all the robberies, over one hundred men were killed protecting and traveling along this road. This gang was a hard one to shut down. Records say that it took a posse of five hundred men to catch the outlaw gang.

A couple of years later, after committing many murders and crimes, they finally met their match. Over twenty four outlaws were shot and killed during the manhunt and the leader, Henry, was finally caught. He stood trial in court and was later hung. History states that over five thousand people show up on the day of the hanging to witness his death. That was a huge turnout back in those days. The twist is some say the posse formed was the actual crime doers and that the gang was only responsible for a few crimes. This posse was called the Vigilante Committee of Virginia City.

Tom Bell Gang—California Territory (1850s)

Dr. Thomas Hodges was an educated man that was born in Alabama and joined the U.S. Army to fight in the Mexican War. He was a man of many talents and some say he stood over six feet tall and was a leader by nature. Later he was named Outlaw Doc and this name is still known today. After the war was over, he traveled west to seek his fortune in gold mining during the California Gold Rush era. He tried his luck in gambling but decided he wasn't good at it either. After some crimes he committed, he was arrested and spent five years in prison. Serving time, he met other outlaws and once they were released, the Tom Bell Gang was created.

This gang was known for robbing travelers, salons, wagons, and more. They held up a stagecoach, carrying one hundred thousand dollars' worth of gold bars but met their match in a gunfight. They were unsuccessful in stealing the gold but a posse was formed to hunt after the gang for the attempt. One by one, the gang members were hunted down and arrested. The gang members that didn't go quietly, were shot and killed. By the time the posse caught up to Tom, he was already hung by the law in Nevada City.

The Cow Boys, aka The Clanton Gang—Arizona and Mexico Territory (1870s-1880s)

This gang was known for the red sashes they wear around their hips. The Clanton family was a gang of family members and their hired hands. The territory was wild without the presence of law for many years. This gang would rob just about this thing that had a prize to be won. This gang was known for many crimes and murders but they were also ranchers as well. For a few years, Sheriff Johnny Behan stayed clear of the Clanton Gang. He never arrested them for any crimes.

Once the Earp brothers and Doc Holliday arrived at Tombstone, things began to change. Virgil Earp accepted the job of Marshal and he decided to make a stand against the Clantons. The Cow Boys were not accustomed to the law and they pushed back. The Earp brothers and Doc Holliday stood at the OK Corral on October 26, 1881. This was the start of a killing spree between both parties. The Earp Brothers lost their youngest brother Morgan during a shooting one night. The Clantons lost some of their family members too. This led to a long bloody battle that reached many outside areas of Tombstone.

The Ketchum Gang—New Mexico Territory (Late 1890s)

The Ketchum gang ended like many other gangs did, arrested, shot, and dead. This gang was started by two brothers, Black Jack Thomas and Sam Ketchum. They formed a gang and one of the members rode with the Wild Bunch later in history. His name was Ben Kilpatrick. Three years went by and the gang worked mostly together robbing post offices, businesses, and trains. One day three gang members committed a robbery without the rest of the gang.

Even Though they were successful in stealing fifty thousand dollars, a posse was formed to hunt down the men.

This was the undoing of the Ketchum Gang and even the gang members that weren't involved with that exact robbery were all treated the same as no good outlaws. Many of them were gunned down and killed and some of them were wounded and managed to get away. Sam Ketchum was shot and later died of blood poisoning. Two other gang members went to trial and were sentenced to life in prison. Carver and Kilpatrick decided to join the Wild Bunch and Butch Cassidy. Black Jack Ketchum was the last member and he decided to rob a train and was shot and arrested. He stood trial in the local courthouse where he was sentenced to death by hanging.

The Red Jack Gang—Arizona Territory (Early 1880s)

This gang was known for robbing stagecoaches along the San Pedro River. This territory was much like Tombstone, there wasn't much law enforcement in the area, and it made it easy for bandits to do what they wanted. The leader of this gang was named Red Jack, aka Jack Averill. The gang robbed a stagecoach in 1883 and it was a Wells Fargo Wagon. When the stagecoach was stopped by the outlaws, one of the appointed Wells Fargo guards told the gang right away that the coach had nothing to steal.

After a dispute, the leader Jack knew that under that seat of the wagon, were concealed gold bars. The guardsman reached for his gun but one of the gang members was quicker. The guard was shot and killed and the gang made off with over three thousand dollars of gold. A posse was formed and the gang was tracked down. One by one the gang members were killed by the posse because the outlaws would not go without a fight. The posse finally tracked down the last gang member, Jack Averill at the gang's hideout near Wilcox Arizona. Jack was also gunned down by the posse and they never found the gold from the robbery. Many locals believe the gold is buried somewhere by the hideout.

—◦—

The Jack Taylor Gang—Arizona and Mexico Territory (1884-1888)

This gang had a leader that was known to be an expert in train robberies and his name was Jack Taylor. This gang was known as a cruel bunch and it caught the attention of a few good lawmen who wanted to stop the crimes and murders completely. The Jack Taylor gang was known for shooting the train's engineers and that was something that was not normal for that time period. In 1887, sheriff Slaughter was informed of the gang members' names and possible whereabouts. The sheriff's posse tracked down two gang members in Contention City Arizona and shot one outlaw as the other escaped.

Later, the Mexican Rurales caught some of the gang members and sentenced them to life in prison. The other gang members on the run were shot and killed and the leader, Jack, was the last one to die.

—◦—

Alvord Stiles Gang—Arizona Territory (1899-1903)

Arizona was a rough western state and many outlaws were known in history; the Alvord Stiles Gang was no exception. This gang was formed by two lawmen who decided to break the law as an outlaw was better than wearing a badge. Burton Alvord was the head leader and spent a lot of time in the saloons. Before he knew it, he became friends with outlaws and decided to form a gang. The gang committed several train robberies and made off with thousands of dollars.

At a later time, one of the outlaws was arrested by the law and Billy Stiles came to his rescue. He held a gun out to the marshal's head, demanding that he let the gang member go. Billy shoots the marshal point blank in the foot. Arizona Rangers hunted and tracked down the gang in Mexico territory and surrounded them. Some of the gang members were killed and a few were imprisoned. One of the outlaws managed to escape the posse and some say that he was seen in Nevada many years later.

Musgrove Gang—Wyoming and Colorado Territory (1860s-1868)

Lewis H. Musgrave was an outlaw and was known as being a genuinely bad guy. Lewis killed a man just because he didn't agree with his political views about the Civil War. He then killed several more in Nevada. He formed a gang that robbed government livestock in Wyoming and Colorado. His gang also traveled to the surrounding states if a herd of cattle was known to be around. It was said during the time of stealing cattle, his gang would shoot and kill anyone that got in their way.

A train was robbed in Elk Mountain Wyoming and the Musgrove Gang put the blame on the local Indian tribe. Some of the gang members were arrested and the free-of-charge members continued the argument in court that Indians robbed the train, killed innocent people, and stole a hundred thousand dollars' worth of livestock. The townspeople were fed up and took matters into their own hands. They broke into the jail and dragged Lewis into the street. Lewis asked if he could write his family members a letter. They agreed and after he was done, they hung in. This was a rough group of outlaws and this goes to show that a good person will fight back against bandits and murders.

SIX

Famous Lawmen and Do-Gooders

We've all heard about the famous stories of outlaws, killing, stealing, and gunfights but what about the people and lawmen that stood up to the outlaws? I would like to tell some of these stories. I think by doing this, you can see that there's always another side to a coin. If the outlaws were out of control, someone had to protect the towns-people and valuables. It's a similar story much like today. If our streets were full of crime and murders, how could we move on with our lives and keep our families safe?

There were many people that stood up to the outlaws. Some of them are well known figures of the old west and some are not. Some of them were more of the rougher type of lawmen or do-gooders and some of them had a darker side to them as well. To my surprise, I found that many lawmen turned to the dark side of crime. After digging into the old western history and lawmen and outlaws, I found that more sheriffs and marshals worked as lawmen for several years and then turned their life around 180 degrees and became an outlaw. There are also some people in history that were more in the middle of the two, good and bad. Let's start off with a man named John Henry Holliday. He is known as Doc Holliday in history and was known for being around during several historical events.

John Henry Holliday, known as Doc Holliday (1851-1887)

There are several interesting things about him and I would like to share that with you. When Doc Holliday was fifteen years old, he lost his mother to tuberculosis, and it took a toll on the young man. His father was a decorated war man and his family was looked up to in the community of Pennsylvania. After having a somewhat rough teenage life, Doc was involved in college where he studied to become a dentist. He had several years of college under his belt and this made him an educational man. Doc spent the next few years practicing dental work in several states. He had a few of his own offices and made a good life of money.

Not long into this life, he was told by doctors that he had contracted tuberculosis, the same disease that killed his mother. From this point on, you can say that he lived his life carefree. In a way, he didn't care so much about the simple things in life. He moved to Texas and met Bat Masterson and worked under a dentist for a short time. Doc's health was declining, and he knew it. It seemed to have been heavy on his mind and his coughing just got worse and worse. As his health fell, he became more and more of a drunk and some would say he made choices as a criminal would. Doc became a heavy drinker and gambler. He spent many nights in saloons, playing the piano, playing poker, and getting into intelligent conversations.

His education would come across as arrogant. It was not as common back in those days for someone to speak Latin, cite books and historical accounts, and go deep into conversations as he did. His drinking and poker playing managed to get him in the heat of the moment with many outlaws and gunfighters. Doc had his fair share of gunfights and shootings. He was arrested several times and for a while, seemed to be known as an outlaw. Some say that when he met Mary Catherine Elder (Big Nose Kate) they became a couple and sometimes would get into many fights that forced stabbings onto others and shootings. When fights broke out, it's claimed that

Doc and Kate would rob the tables of money as they left town. The two spent a lot of time going from town to town. Doc was heading west because he was told by doctors that the dry climate might help him live longer.

When he arrived in Tombstone, Arizona, that's where he was once again joined by his good friend Wyatt Earp. You know that story about the OK Corral now and those events. Doc was appointed deputy marshal with Earp's consent and that's the only time Doc was a lawman, helping Earp track down and kill the Cow Boys of Tombstone. During all of Doc's history of possible questionable acts, he was only involved in 8 shootouts. Today in history he is well known and liked by many. Wyatt Earp enjoyed his company and I think that's what kept Doc somewhat in line. I would say the Doc was a bad, good guy. He was liked by many. This is a good story that shows and explains the difference between then and now.

———————— ◦ ————————

Horace Bell—Los Angeles (1830-1918)

Horace was known to be a good, good guy of the law. He went to college in Kansas and learned many things, including how to become a lawyer. In his life, he was a soldier, lawyer, journalist, and published author of two books. In 1850, he decided to leave Kentucky and move to California because of the gold rush that took place there. He tried his hand at learning how to prospect and gold pan, but he didn't have much luck with it. He did try mining for about years but decided to give it up. Due to his experiences with the law, he joined the Los Angeles Rangers. His militia was known for going after some of the worst outlaws, commenting on some of the worst crimes.

After taking on that role for a while, he did join the Army and did pretty good for himself and became a Major in Walker Fili-buster's army. Later in his life, he joined Benito Juarez's army in Mexico and fought in the Reform War, and later joined the Union Army during the Civil War. He had a lot of war experience behind him. In 1866, he married and had children and they decided to move back to Los Angeles. He then worked as a lawyer and journalist. He did his part in his county, and he was known to have arrested many outlaws and enforced the law.

Lawmen like him made a difference and helped keep the west safer from bad people and gangs. Horace died on June 29th of 1918 and was buried in Rosedale Cemetery. His two books are called *Reminiscences of a Ranger: Early Times in Southern California* and *On the Old West Coast: Being Further Reminiscences of a Ranger*.

N. K. Boswell—Laramie Wyoming (1841-1904)

His full name was Nathaniel Kimball Boswell and he was known as a cattleman, rancher, Cow Boy, and lawman. He was a private man when it came to politics and history is undecided if he fought for the Union or the Confederate army in the Civil War. He moved to Laramie Wyoming to meet with his brother George Boswell and his family. They arrived right at the beginning of the town and became one of the first settlers there. After some time the area grew wild and rough due to the lack of law. Many outlaws moved into the area and started to pull the same as we've all heard before, robberies, shootings, and murders.

Nathaniel quickly became a part of the Vigilance Committee in the hopes that he can help keep his family and land safe from outlaws. Later, he and his brother opened a saloon and went into business for themselves.

Pat Garrett—New Mexico Territory (1850-1908)

This is another good lawman but if he wasn't connected with Billy the Kid, his name may not have been remembered in history. He was known as a bartender, buffalo hunter, customs agent, and family man in his life. Pat was known as a trusted man that worked along with the conservative side of Lincoln County. He never fully trusted Billy the Kid; he did allow him in the community until the Lincoln County War broke out. John Chisum was a powerful cattleman and land owner of the area and Pat worked for him until he was appointed Sheriff. During this time, Billy and Pat did work alongside on a few tasks.

He was known as a bartender, buffalo hunter, customs agent, and family man in his life. Pat is most famous for killing Billy the Kid and his pursuit of ending the war. Pat spent almost a year tracking down Billy's gang of regulators one by one. This was a very complicated time for the area and most people involved were trying to do what they thought was right. Pat did the same when he was hiding in the shallows in a bedroom. Billy woke during the night when he was staying at Maxwell's house. Billy got out of bed and Pat was waiting for him in the dark and that's where Pat fired his gun twice, killing the kid.

After the war, Pat moved to Texas where he became a Texas Ranger. Pat's life continued like this for over nineteen years. Even then Pat was killed in the line of duty. In many ways, Pat was a celebrated lawman and he should be remembered for that in the years to come.

David J. Cook—Denver Colorado (1842-1907)

David was a Marshall for the Denver Colorado area and was responsible for over three thousand arrests in his career. Before he was an accomplished lawman, he worked as a farmhand for several years in Kansas. After that, he tried his hand at striking it rich as a miner, looking for gold. In 1862, he joined the Colorado Cavalry during the Civil War. His job was tracking down spies of the Confederate army and investigating gold smugglers. Later he moved on to working for the Pinkerton Agency.

At one point he was working as a marshal and acting as a federal marshal detective. Lastly, he was involved in the revolt of the Ute tribe in Colorado. His ambitious life as a lawman explained how dedicated he was to enforcing what he thought was right and the law. The last job he worked was as an arbitrator at the silver mine in Leadville. He died of natural causes and was buried at the Riverside Cemetery. His name has been remembered over the years, just like it should. David showed courage and grit in a time when he had to be strong to make a difference.

Bass Reeves—Arkansas and Oklahoma Territory (1838-1910)

Bass Reeves was the first black deputy marshal in the historical records, west of the Mississippi River. He was by far a very good lawman, even though history has forgotten him. He was born in July of 1838 and died on January 12th, 1910. It's said that he may have been the man that inspired the movie caricature, the Lone Ranger.

Bass was a serious lawman. He was born in Arkansas territory during the time that slaves were being used in the area. By the time he was eight years old, Bass was moved to Texas. His owner, William Steele Reeves, did give him fair treatment, differently than most of his slaves. He taught Bass how to read and write which placed him in a different bracket than the others. When Bass was a teenager, William placed Bass in charge of the armory in and around the plantation and Bass learned his way around firearms. When the Civil War broke out, Reeves took Bass with him in war to fight alongside him.

When Bass had the chance, he escaped the war and got away from Reeves, and never looked back. He lived with the local Indians of Oklahoma. This area back then was called the Indian Territory. After a couple of years went by, Bass was now a man and he wanted to find a job that he was good at. He was a new husband and father and he had to provide for his family. He knew that area very well and many of the men were out fighting the war. At this time, Bass was offered a job as a U.S. deputy marshal.

He became a known tracker. Outlaws started to fear him because Bass was devoted to bringing in wanted men. Over his career, he arrested three-thousand outlaws and bandits. He was smart. He wouldn't introduce himself as a lawman. He would act as if he was an outlaw too. This way, he could deceive the wanted men and when they weren't looking, he put the handcuffs on them and took them to jail to pay for their crimes.

Bass did not like killing wanted outlaws. He did his best to keep them alive. He was known as a religious man and he stuck to his morals. So much, his own son killed his wife for being unfaithful to him. Bass received the warrant for his son and arrested him. His son was tried and sentenced to prison. Bass was in many gunfights. They say that he was very good and quick with his guns. Bass retired from the law and he lived out his life a happy man. When he passed away, it's said that many people came to his funeral. He was well respected.

For some reason, he was not shown in Hollywood movies and history doesn't mention him much. He accomplished more than many of the top ten lawmen of the old west. I figured that not only would I write about him in this book, but I also want to give him a round of applause. Being a black man during the time of the Civil war would have been hard. Acting as a black lawman would have been very hard as well.

Allan Pinkerton (1819-1884)

If you were thinking it, yes, Allan was the founder of the Pinkerton National Detective Agency. Allan was a wood craftsman for some time, making barrels and wagon wheels. He spent a lot of time in the wilderness and this is how the Pinkertons were invented. He was out in the woods and was soon observing a group of people. He stayed back and watched the activities of this group and later learned that it was the Banditti of the Prairie (Pirates of the Prairie) gang. It went into town to tell the local sheriff of their whereabouts and the gang was arrested. He was offered the job of a police detective and that's what led to the creation of the Pinkerton organization.

After some time serving as a detective, he decided that he wanted to start his own agency and took on a partner, Edward Rucker. They both invested their money and soon later, Allan was working for himself. Later the Pinkerton Company grew to be a force to be reckoned with. It solved many train robberies and started to take on more private jobs protecting stagecoaches and tracking down outlaws. Soon Securitas was a branch of the Pinkerton company, which is the largest security company in the modern day world. The Pinkerton Company and Agency made a huge impact in the west by cracking down on outlaws.

Even Abraham Lincoln visited Allan and his organization many times. Even Butch Cassidy and the Wild Bunch was chased by the Pinkertons which led to some of the hardship Butch had in his criminal life. I worked for Securitas as a regional manager for a few years while I was going to Dixie University. This is where I learned about the history of the Pinkertons. Securitas still holds pride in its legacy today. If it wasn't for Allan's pursuit and detective work, it's very possible that the west would have been a rougher place to live for many more years than it was.

We can't forget the other lawmen of the west. I've mentioned many in this book. I would like to once again mention Wyatt Earp, Bat Masterson, and many more that deserve recognition as well. I don't think the world will ever get rid of evil and that's why it's so important to have good guys. The balance of life will remain, and I hope that many more do-gooders will fall in line and go down in history, just like some of the men I've mentioned above. I hope by mentioning the names that I have; you'll continue your search to learn more about the lawmen that helped make America the way it is today.

SEVEN

Billy the Kid and the Regulator Gang

Billy the Kid Tintype

This story of the old west could possibly be one of the most famous. Hollywood and the entertainment industry have created a lot of movies and written accounts of Billy the Kid. I want to tell the story from a historical researcher's point of view. Billy was twenty-one years old when he was killed, hints the nickname "Kid". He was involved with murders and other criminal activities before the famous legend of the Lincoln County War in the New Mexico territory. Here's his story.

Henry McCarty (Billy the Kid) was born in 1859 and was also known as William H. Bonney, later known as Billy the Kid. In this chapter, I'll refer to him as "Billy" and/or "Billy the Kid." Billy's parents were from an Irish Catholic past and Billy was baptized in Saint Peter's Church in Manhattan, New York. His baptism records are on file with the church with his parents' names, his name, and the date, September 28, 1959. His birth parents were Patrick McCarty and Catherine Devine. His family lived in the New York area for some time until his father passed away. After his father's death, Catherine decided to move away to start a new life. They traveled to Indianapolis Indiana and started to live their lives once again.

Catherine met a man named William Henry Harrison Antrim and they started their courtship, and the relationship grew. The McCarty family moved to Wichita, Kansas, in 1870 and three years later, Antrim and Catherine were married. Shortly after that event, the new family picked up once again to move to Santa Fe New Mexico. Unfortunately, Catherine died of tuberculosis on September 16, 1874. Billy had now lost both his birth parents and that's when Billy's behavior changed. Antrim was not a perfect stepfather to the kids and the McCarty brothers ended up in a boarding home very shortly after their mom's death.

Some claim that was the last straw for Billy. Shortly afterward, the McCarty brother was caught stealing food, and then ten days later, they robbed a Chinese laundry mat. They took clothing and two guns were taken. The boys were caught and put in jail for the crimes. This was the first time in history that Billy was published. The Silver City Herald wrote an article about the boy's wrongdoings. Two days later the brothers escaped from jail. Billy took his brother, Joseph McCarty with him and they tracked down their stepfather Antrim. At this point in time, Billy and Joseph were fugitives, who were wanted boys by the law. They found their stepfather's home and asked to stay with him but once Antrim caught word of the boy's crimes, he kicked them out of his home.

During the argument, Billy stuffed some clothes and guns into a bag before Antrim threw the boys out the front door. This was the last time the boys ever saw their stepfather. Nothing was ever mentioned in history about his brother Joseph and what happened to him but Billy was on the run and he ended up in Arizona territory. He found work as a ranch hand and traded from employer to employer for some time. Billy became a gambler during his off time from work. He also started making friends with outlaws and men who were on the wrong side of the law. He met a man named John R. Mackie and the two started stealing horses in the Camp Grant area of Arizona.

On August 17th, 1877, Billy was at a saloon and got into a fight with Francis Cahill, a blacksmith from the area. It was known that Cahill bullied Billy around and that night, Billy had enough of it. The two ended up on the floor of the saloon and so did Billy's gun. Both men struggled to reach for the gun, fighting off each other at the same time. Billy was the first to grab his revolver and he shot Cahill. His wounds did not heal and the following day, Cahill was dead. There was a witness to the fight and he claimed that it was a fair fight, Billy shot Cahill in self-defense. Billy fled the area and a man named Miles Wood arrested him and took him to the Camp Grants guardhouse.

Before law enforcement arrived to transfer Billy as a prisoner, he escaped once again. The newspapers wrote about this event and Billy had no choice but to leave the Arizona territory. He stole a horse and made his way back to the New Mexico state line. During his ride, Apaches met up with Billy and stole the horse from him. I guess that goes to show you what the life of an outlaw was like back then. Billy was forced to walk miles and miles until he came to the closest settlement which was called Fort Station in Pecos Valley. Billy found his friend's house which was owned by one of the gang members of the Seven Rivers Warriors. His name was John Jones.

John's mother found Billy in a state of near death and nursed him back to wealth. Billy was dying of starvation and dehydration. It took some time but Billy did get his health back and before he knew it, he joined a band of cattle rustlers that raided a herd of cattle owned by John Chisum, the wealthy land and cattleman of the New Mexico territory. Billy was seen in Silver City with these cattle rustlers and once again, Billy was branded an outlaw in the newspapers. At this point in his life, Billy was known as William H. Bonney. He finally had a chance to change his ways. It was seen by a businessman named John Henry Tunstall who made a habit of taking in and hiring young men that had a hard childhood.

John Tunstall was a good man with many business ventures that acquired men like Bill and his gunfighting skills. When Billy was brought to John's ranch home, Billy was surrounded by others like him but this time, this group was more refined. John took in several men that he kept at his home and cared for them. He worked them during the day, fed and housed them at night. John was the kind of man that would teach these boys life lessons, clothed them, and even taught them how to read. He was well known in the area as a good man. He was strict with Billy but he was the first person to show any concern for Billy since his mother passed away.

John and Billy's relationship grew over time. John even took Billy into town to buy him clothes. John told Billy that it was an advance from his first paycheck. Billy admired John very much and the more John showed kindness to Billy, the more Billy started to change for the better. Bill learned that the other men at John's home were called the Regulators. John hired them to help out around that ranch and to go after cattle rustlers or any other outlaws that would steal him. John would send his regulators out to use the full extinction of the law to regain his property back. Billy wasn't allowed to help the Regulators at first. He was kept at the ranch to help in other ways. John believed the law had to be used and practiced within the boundaries. Even if his band of regulations went after outlaws, he made sure that it wasn't an act of hate or criminality.

This is where Billy started to learn that bad people and outlaws cause harm to good people in ways of emotional and financial burdens. For the first time in a while, Billy was on the right side of the fence. John was well respected by many people in the area. The townspeople and law enforcement knew that John handled events in a good manner. Even though Billy was in a good crowd, it seemed to be hard to escape his crimes from the past. Many people in the Lincoln County knew about Billy's outlaw activities and the murder he committed in Arizona.

This is where I want to explain some of my opinions about Billy and his new situation. Even though Billy was a known bandit, I wonder if it wasn't due to losing his parents and being cast away by his stepfather. I'm going to explain a little. It's easy to say that all younger men that commit unlawful acts can be tied to their childhood, but I feel that Billy's situation was a little different. Billy wasn't like most of the Regulators he was surrounded by at John's House. Billy was able to read and write. Most of the Regulators couldn't until John taught them. When people first met Billy during this time in life, he didn't seem to be a murderer. His personality was quiet and not mean.

It appears to me that Billy wasn't neglected in his childhood like some of the Regulators. In my opinion, Billy was raised by his mom to be a good man and Christian. This is why he attended school until his mom died. This is why he wasn't a troublemaker until he seemed to be broken by unfortunate events in his life. I believe that he was a broken hearted kid that had nothing and that's why he turned to the life of crime. I would say at the age of fifteen, he may not have had much choice. The first time he got into trouble with the law was because he was stealing food and clothes. The murder people said he committed, was a man who bullied him for quite a while.

He stole a horse to get out of town. Are these acts of a bad kid or of desperation? Maybe even an emotional kid, keeping his feelings inside. Keep this in mind as I explain more of the story and history of Billy the Kid. During the time that Billy worked with John, he met many people in the surrounding area. John knew many and Billy even met the man he stole cattle from earlier, John Chisum. Billy started to get acquainted with good working people. The more Billy started to change in the right direction, the more John allowed him to get more involved with his affairs and business. Billy was known in town and even though people were standoffish towards him, people respected John and in return, they tried their best to accept Billy's presence.

There was one man that John did not like and for good reason, Lawrence Murphy. Billy's first encounter with Murphy was when he accused John of stealing from him by using his group of Regulators to rob his wagons of supplies meant for his stores and businesses. John was approached by Murphy and the sheriff of the town and the fingers were pointed at John and his Regulators. John explained to the sheriff that they had no proof it was his Regulators and the changes went dismissed for the time being. Billy learned from John that Murphy used his name and money in the area to stop competition that could pose a threat to his businesses. John received a government contract at the time Murphy was causing trouble and his motives seemed loud and clear to John and Billy.

Nothing in town would happen unless Murphy allowed it. His company managed and regulated what businesses could be started and some say Murphy used his money and power to control law enforcement. John is the kind of man he was, telling Billy to leave it alone. For some time, Billy did. Murphy wasn't just disliked by John Tunstall, but John Chisum didn't like him at all, either. Chisum was known as a large landowner and even a bigger cattleman. John and Murphy did not get along and Chisum was a man that didn't take this kind of behavior kindly. Chisum was known as a fighter, a gunman, and a man that would stand up for what is right. Chisum also had many employees that were good with guns, like the Regulators but with less hoodlum type of demeanor.

Billy felt more and more like a part of a family once again, attending dances and get-togethers in town. Some would say that Billy was a changed man. Pat Garrett and Billy met at one of these town dances. Pat knew of Billy's reputation and never had much to say to him at first. Pat was making a name for himself and was hired by Chisum at the time, and he wasn't comfortable being around Billy. It wasn't until John and Chisum decided to go into business with each other and open a general store that Pat and Billy got to know each other better. John and Chisum were both businessmen and they wanted to start pushing Murphy out of power by creating businesses in town. Murphy at this point owns many businesses but John and Chisum wanted to change that.

There were situations where Billy and Pat were put on the same task of protecting some supplies coming into town that John and Chisum ordered to stock their soon-to-be store. This angered Murphy but Chisum did not hesitate to fight back. John tried to persuade Chisum from doing anything to Murphy, other than competing in business. That didn't work too well. Chisum and Murphy even got into an argument one day and Chisum punched him right in front of the whole town. At this point, Murphy paid off the sheriff's department and now, he could do almost anything he wanted. Chisum wasn't about to let up and John was convinced they needed to bring in their own law from out of town.

John asked Chisum to wait and hold off any more fighting with Murphy until he brought back some lawyers and law enforcement to their town. John hopped on his horse carriage and headed out of town. After several miles on the road, Murphy's persuaded lawman caught up to John. They told him that he was going to be arrested and taken back to town. John insisted that they left him alone until he came back. The lawmen shot and killed John wrongfully right there, in his carriage. Then they planted a gun on him and claimed that John tried to shoot them. Chisum, Billy, Pat, and the Regulators knew better and so the Lincoln County War began. This was truly a time of right and wrong. Good versus evil. Business against business.

The one thing that everyone didn't see coming is how Billy was going to act about his friend and mentor's murder. Chisum sent his men, including Pat Garrett to retrieve the crooked lawmen back to town to stand trial for their wrongdoing. Murphy did his best to hide these men out of sight. Chisum was a brave and stubborn man, and he didn't stop until they found the murderers that killed John. Because of Billy's emotions, Chisum asked Billy to stay out of the affairs until they were captured and jailed. Billy did what he thought was right. He told Pat and Chisum that he would but by the time Pat and Chisum's men arrested the murderers, Billy was hiding in the distance.

While Pat and his men were riding back into town, Billy caught them by surprise and shot and killed the men that killed John. Pat couldn't do anything but stand back and watch. Even though Billy won that battle in his mind, he wanted to hurt the man that he felt responsible for John's death, Mr. big-time businessman Murphy. Everyone knew Murphy was to blame and his boughten law was out of control but now Billy made Chisum's side look bad. Pat, Chisum, and others tried to talk Billy out of the violence, but Billy and the Regulators wanted revenge and wouldn't stop at anything to get it. Billy and the Regulators were deputized to hunt down more of

Murphy's crooked lawmen but that just made things worse. Even though Bill and his posse were winning the battle, Murphy was winning the war.

One by one, Billy's posse met up with Murphy's men. Billy was using his badge to justify his killings. Murphy used the law to bring in more law and soon Billy and his Regulators were the wanted men. Chisum and Pat had no choice but to tell Billy that he was wrong. They tried to remind him that John would have wanted him to conduct this situation with the court systems. Once again, Billy was a wanted man. He lost the support of Pat Garrett and John Chisum but that didn't stop the Regulators.

At this point, Murphy was in contact with the State of New Mexico. He told the Mayor and Governor that Chisum was a criminal and that Billy and the Regulators were killing the law nonstop. The more law that came into town, the more the Regulators fought back. Billy and his gang would kill every lawman that stood in their way. Billy was now called Billy the Kid in the local newspapers.

Chisum did stand down from the fight. Not because he wanted to but because Billy and his gang were in the wrong. The gang wasn't killing for what was right at this point, it was pure revenge for John. Billy's gang did try to get away and head west to escape but Billy was a man that convinced them to stay and fight. This decision was the death of the Regulators but not until they caused more deaths. The Regulators stayed in Lincoln County and tried to get back at Murphy as much as they could. They robbed and killed his men bringing in supplies into town.

They held up his carriages full of money so they could rob him. They figured that if they could keep this up, then it would break Murphy. The Regulators did everything they could and every time they went into town, a gunfight broke out. The Governor of Lincoln County put bounties on the Regulator's heads. Wanted posters were put up and two hundred dollars were placed on Billy's head, dead or alive. Chisum's lawyers tried to reach out to the President of the United States but the Governor was corrupted by Murphy too. There wasn't much hope in Lincoln County and the Regulators and Murphy's gang were left to fight it out themselves.

Some of the Regulators were killed one by one but Billy wasn't ready to stop until his gang was dead or until Murphy and his gang was dead. At this time, Pat Garrett was appointed Sheriff of the area to stop the killing and battle that has been going on for months and months. Because Billy and Pat became somewhat of friends, Pat met with Billy to tell him that Murphy's gang arrested Chisum's lawyer and that they would kill him unless the Regulators give themselves up. Billy and the Regulators rode off to help the lawyer and arrived at his house the next day. An ambush was in play and as the Regulators were in the lawyer's home, Murphy's gang surrounded it. This stand-off lasted overnight and even the Calvary showed up.

They were on Murphy's side of the course because Murphy's bought and persuaded everyone. Many men were killed during this standoff. During the getaway, the regulators were killed except for a couple. Even the lawyer was shot down in the street. The one thing that was accomplished by the Regulators that day is Billy was given the opportunity to kill Murphy. He shot him as he was leaving town. Regulators that were still alive after this event, split off and went their separate ways. Many things at this time changed in the county. The mayor was forced to resign and be replaced. Murphy's company did fall and was closed soon after the war. The lawyer's wife continued with John and Chisum's plan and she became one of the most successful cattlewomen in New Mexico.

The Regulators were done. The ones that lived changed their name and still today, only a few may have known their true identity. Billy the Kid never left New Mexico. This was his undoing after Pat Garrett became sheriff. During the night, Pat was hiding in the shadows of a home Billy was staying at. When Billy got up in the middle of the night, Pat shot and killed Billy. Pat went on to become a great lawman. The battle was over but the history and spirit of the fight still remain.

If I lived in this area today, I would do all I could to learn the locations of the points of interest. Billy and the Regulators robbed much of Murphy's supplies and money during this time.

If someone was to narrow down some locations, they might be able to not only find rich lost historical artifacts, but they could also be lucky enough to find some of the money, gold, and silver. I know for a fact that the Regulators kept some of the money, but I also know that they were on the run and didn't stay in many places for very long. They didn't have much time to spend the money and they were not reported in town very often. When they were, there usually was a fight, leaving little time to do something with the money. I suspect that much of it was buried in remote places outside of town. If you checked into it, you could make a great discovery and possibly find new lost history.

I will write more about the possibilities of finding lost locations and buried loot in this story later. I explain how to look for and find lost historical reports, maps, and locations. It'll also teach you how to look for clues to lost treasures in the field.

EIGHT

Butch Cassidy and the Castle Gate Robbery

I want to use this chapter, not only to give some history and shed some light on Butch Cassidy and the Wild Bunch but to compare differences. The difference between researching in the office or in school compared to real-life fieldwork. In 2017, I was contacted by a well-known film producer. They asked me what I knew about Butch Cassidy's history and the treasures he left behind. At the time, I explained to them that I knew about many treasures, but I wasn't the expert on Butch Cassidy.

They explained to me that they were going to do a pilot tv series with Chris Jericho, the famous wrestler. They also mentioned that they were looking for the right treasure hunting team to take him into the wilderness. Hopefully, a team that could possibly find some lost history and riches. I explained to them that I wouldn't do it without my team. I then told them something like this couldn't be done with just a couple of guys. It was going to take a lot of manpower and equipment. We talked about this idea over the phone for the next couple of weeks. Going over ideas and what we should focus on we decided to reach out to people that have experience in researching old western history.

One phone call led to another and I had the pleasure of speaking with many great people and historians that were eager to work with us. Many of them shared information with us that helped point us in the right direction. I also had a talk with my father in law, Dean Dopp and I asked him a few questions about the old west. He was born in Northern Utah and then moved to the Malad area of Idaho at a young age. He was born in 1940 and grew up in these small towns. He told me that there was one story that always came up in conversations about outlaws and old western stories and legends when he was going up. Butch Cassidy and the Wild Butch stories were widely known in the area he grew up. He told me that the most famous story was about the gang's hideout, Robbers Roost.

He said that if someone could find their hangout, the possibilities of many historical discoveries would be very high. At a later time, my team and I did find Robbers Roost and I'll explain more about that in this chapter. Within a couple of weeks, we decided to start looking into the Castle Gate Robbery that Butch Cassidy and Elzy Lay committed. There were a few reasons why we decided to hunt after this story and treasure. For starters, Castle Gate is a ghost town at this point in time. It was a mining town. Second, the information that we discovered suggested that the outlaws took the stolen goodies to their hideout southeast of where the crime took place.

Third, this robbery was one of the riskiest robberies still recorded today because it was done with two people, in broad daylight. It wasn't strange for the Wild Bunch to pull off crimes with a small group of people, but this idea was just plain crazy. That's why they figured it was going to work. No one was expecting it. Let me explain. Castle Gate was a mining town. Many people that lived there were either miners themselves or everyday townspeople. Pleasant Valley Coal Company was a large company that spent paper money, gold, and silver coins on the train to Castle Gate to pay their employees.

This payroll was a scheduled stop for the train route and the coal mining employees were paid about every two weeks. Butch and Elzy scouted the routine of the town for a few weeks. After observing the behavior of the town they noticed that the payroll duffle bags were carried from the train to the main office building every time. They also felt that the armed men appeared too comfortable, almost like they were expecting any kind of trouble.

Butch and Elzy decided that a plan to steal the payroll could be easy, as far as simply taking the bags from the guards and heading out of town. After more consideration, they were relieved that the location and getting out of town were going to be the most difficult part. Not only did they have to figure out where to keep their horses in town for a quick getaway they also had to consider that a posse would be right behind them once the robbery took place. Butch was a good horseman, and he thought his idea of setting up horses every few miles out of town, would be a good idea.

Butch figured that if a posse chased them, both group's horses would start to slow down and get tired after a few miles. Butch and Elzy decided to set up groups of two horses, every few miles, along the trail they would use to escape. This way the posses horse would start getting tired and Butch and Elzy could trade for fresh new horses. This would create more space between the outlaws and the law. Butch and Elzy trained for a couple more weeks and got their horses and guns ready. What happened on the day of the robbery would be remembered in history for a very long time. Before the train came into town, a lone cowboy tied up his horse at a saloon.

This cowboy went into the saloon and sat down, not ordering anything and that caught the attention of a couple of people, including the bartender. As soon as the train coasted slowly into town, the train blew its whistle and that's when the cowboy got up and walked away from his table. He made his way down towards the train station. He was seen standing back at a distance, watching the passengers and suppliers getting unloaded from the train. At the same time as this situation, another man was seen, lingering around the staircase of the coal mining company office.

The stairway headed up to a second-story office where the Coal Company conducted business matters. The company's employees were making their way from the train to the office, carrying duffle bags that the employee's payroll was sealed in. These employees consisted of three men, the paymaster, and two guards. Three duffle bags were reported walking down the street towards the office. It is said that the bags contained about seven nine thousand dollars' worth of silver, gold, and paper money. The employees made a turn in the street and were around seventy-five yards from the office when the same lone cowboy pulled out his gun and held up the employees, demanding that they hand over the bags.

The lone man took the biggest bag the paymaster was carrying. Just moments after, the man spotted lingering around the office came up to the same employees and took another bag from them. This all happened in broad daylight. All of this happened so fast that only one person tried to interfere without any luck. A few moments later, a customer saw what was happening and he tried to stop the two cowboys but he was met with a gun, pointed at him and he backed off. Then the two cowboys made their way around the corner of the street and the townspeople were already yelling, they stole the payroll money. Miners and employees were frantically looking where the two cowboys went so, they could get their money back.

Back in those days, if the payroll was robbed, delayed, or an accident happened, they didn't get paid. So the townspeople wanted to stop the thieves from getting away and heading out of town. Because a robbery like this was never done before, everyone in the town was caught off guard. It made it easier for the thieves to get away. The town was in a panic. As the thieves were getting on their horses that were tied up just a few buildings away, two people, one on a buggy and one on a horse were yelling as they chased them, "Bring that money back!" Before anyone really was aware of all the commotion, the thieves were already out of the town, heading in the south direction.

We now know that the two thieves were Butch Cassidy and Elzy Lay. Some people tried to get the sheriff on the phone but realized that the phone lines were cut before the robbery and the law had no idea of what just happened. Remember I said that Butch and Elzy were taking their time, scouting out the town prior to the robbery? This is what they were doing, making notes about how they can stall anyone from chasing them out of town. It worked. The surprise robbery and taking away their communication were brilliant. By the time that a posse was formed, Butch and Elza were several miles out of the town. They had relay horses waiting for them every few miles.

This gave them a huge advantage once again and once the posse tried to track them down, they were even more miles ahead. That wasn't the only smart thing the two outlaws did. They trained their horses to run without horseshoes so the posse would get confused. With no horseshoes, the trackers from the posse assumed that they were tracking wild horses. They never did find the tracks of the outlaws after a few miles. Butch and Elzy made a clean getaway, and they continued heading in the southeast direction. History tells that the two outlaws were heading to the famous Robbers Roost, south of Green River Utah. The gang's hangout was very well hidden and guarded by the gang and the posse and law enforcement had no idea where to look for the gang from that point.

The newspapers were released, and the law was on the lookout for the Wild Bunch, but they had no leads. It was said that a pin was put in the effort to find the gang until they were spotted in Utah. Now the two bags of silver were reported to be around seven thousand dollars' worth. In today's value, that would be around two hundred and fifty thousand dollars of silver and gold. That's a good-sized treasure to find if someone could discover its whereabouts.

Because of the attention, the Wild Butch had on them at this point in time, the Wild Bunch wasn't seen together again.

Some of them headed to separate states and were picked up by the law one by one. Not Butch. It's said that this is when Butch went to Central America to hide. This would be around the same time when he was reported dead after a standoff gunfight. Many Utah residents and local people in the area of Castle Gate and Green River say that the gang must have hidden the silver and gold near their hideout at Robbers Roost. Still today, Utah will claim that the silver and gold is now considered buried treasure, somewhere in the Canyonlands of Utah. This is where the Treasures in America team and myself got involved with this story, almost one hundred and twenty-five years later after the Castle Gate robbery.

In the vicinity of the gang's hideout at Robbers Roost, Canyonlands, Utah

I was at my desk one day in 2017. I received an email from a film company asking me some questions about treasures in Utah state. The email asked me if I knew of some good treasure stories in the area. They said in the email that they are going to make a tv show about lost treasures and have a famous man be the host of it. In the same email, they asked if I was willing to have a phone conversation with them and talk more about it. The email was fairly short and sweet and I thought about it for a couple of minutes and replied with an email back to them, stating that I was interested and what did they have in mind. Within an hour, the film company emailed me back with a link to a phone chat.

I called my team to give them the information and they were

excited to see where this conversation may go. For the next few weeks, I had many conversations with the filming company. They scheduled many phone calls with people that have spent much of their lives, tracking down historical accounts and stories of Butch Cassidy and the Wild Bunch. I was learning a lot but one thing was holding me and my team up—the location. It was so remote that I knew from my past experience with treasure hunting and historical researching, that it would not be an easy task to take on. Equipment and the right tools for the job were going to be one of the hardest tasks to take on. While my team was working on equipment, I was working with the filmmaking company in meetings and helping with the unscripted, scripted writing for the show.

It was a big task to take on. Not only did we want it to be exciting for everyone to watch, but we also had to make sure that we were successful in making some discoveries in the field. This is where I knew that I had to get out of creation mode and go into my explorer and treasure hunting mode. I didn't know much about the area, in fact, I've never been in the Canyonlands of Utah other than passing by on the highway. This posed a big problem for me and my team. How could we make a great TV episode if we didn't know the area? My team and I decided to plan a scouting trip to the area. When it comes to scouting trips, we try to only familiarize ourselves with the landscape.

We don't take much equipment with us, just off-road vehicles to get us around. During a couple of my talks with experts, I was told that there could be two hideouts in the Canyonlands area. One was known as Robbers Roost and one was known as an even more secretive hideout. This second hideout was used if the Wild Butch needed to go deeper into the wilderness to escape the law. We were told that if we could find this second hideout, the possibilities of making a great discovery would be even greater. My team and I did some research by using satellite imaging software and topographic maps of the area. We agreed that these other experts were pointing us to the Goblin Valley State Park area of Utah.

We knew it wouldn't be in the park itself but to the west of the park boundaries. We didn't want to go after Robbers Roost at this time, we wanted to find the second hideout and see what the terrain was like. Shaun, Todd, Antonio, and I hopped in the truck, pulling Shaun's UTV and we got on the highway. It was a five hour drive to Goblin Valley from St. George Utah. It was an interesting drive, to say the least. St. George is a red painted desert and as we headed east towards Circleville Utah, the landscape became green and lush. Within a couple more hours, we find ourselves in a faraway place and desolate desert of the Canyonlands. There are not many towns or service exits from Salina to Green River Utah.

You learn very quickly that you are truly in a place of the world that is still never much explored. Many of the local residents told me that this area still holds many secrets. I can see why as I was driving and admiring the area. At that time, phone service was very bad and if you were lucky enough to get one bar, you better make your phone calls. We finally got to the State Park, and we made a right turn (heading south) and traveled down a dirt road for another forty-five miles until we reached our camping ground. It was dark when we set up and we used the headlights of our vehicles to see as we set up camp. This wasn't unusual for our team. We travel all day and set up camp at night about ninety percent of the time.

Goblin Valley State Park Campsite

The next morning, we woke up to this picture that I took above. The morning air was fresh and cool. We were ready to go and we had a lot of ground to cover at this point. We had no idea what lay ahead but we did know that this hideout was still a seventy-five-mile drive on a dirt road. We packed up the ice cooler, some gear, and food into Shaun's UTV and we were gone. Scouting the area was the task and that wasn't hard to do at all. Before we knew it, we found an area that was mined many years before we came into the area. We found mine entrances, structures, stone houses, and tons of old relics left behind from the old mining days.

We stopped at every place we could to take pictures and explore these sites. Because it was a state park, the buildings were still in pretty good shape and condition. This is a rare thing these days because many places like this get destroyed by man or time and weather. We learned that the area didn't just have one or two mines, there were several mines and buildings, spread out for about a good twenty miles. Although the mines were bared-off with iron, we were still able to hike and explore the area. Some of the mining wooden structures were still standing too. It made for a perfect scouting trip. These are the best kind of trips because we're not only seeking information about the area, but we get to enjoy the old historical sites as well. We were on a mission, so we took pictures and pressed on to the location of the possible hideout, still to the west of where we were.

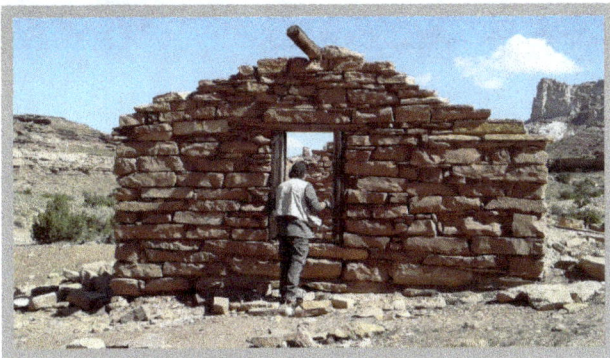

Todd Andersen exploring an old miners' cabin

Shaun Fotheringham at an old storage building

A mining cart wooden ramp and mine dump

When we left the area of the mines, the terrain did change. We went from a low desert-like landscape to what appeared to be more green vegetation and trees. This was what I was told on the phone. This hideout was more in the trees and hidden than Robbers Roost. We travel for another hour down the road, only to find an old trail. It looked like an old horse trail that hasn't been used in many years. Even with our UTV, we had to stop the search for the missing hideout. We continued on foot for as long as we could, but the trail was uphill and continued on for another fifteen miles from where we left the UTV.

We knew that we were defeated at this point. We pulled out the topographic map and figured that this hunt would have to wait for another trip. We would need to come back, set up camp closer to this area, and bring horses. Otherwise, we would not be able to reach the area of the hideout. It was disappointing but we did what I call, the process of elimination. We know what we need for next time. That possibility is still out there to find this supposedly second hideout cabin. We still to this day have not made it back to start off where we left off. We have taken on so many projects that this one would have to wait. When we got back to our hometown, I had another phone conversation with the experts, and they reassured me that it could be positive.

They explained the known Robbers Roost was a winter hideout and the one that we sought after was a summer destination hideout. I think they may be right because where we scouted, where the trail turned into a horse trail, it was much higher in elevation and cooler in temperature. I will leave a summer Robbers Roost (Summer Hideout) hint with you. There are two knoll hills in the Goblin Valley area where it's been said that the second Robbers Roost can be found today. Some old timers say the Butch and his gang released the location to only a few family members in the late 1890s. The clues are mentioned that two knolls were a landscape point for the outlaws to see and ride towards.

This area created a great location where no one traveled back in those days. The hideout had one way in and one way out. If you were to look for two knolls in the Lone Person Hole location, you may be able to find the cabin. The outlaws claimed that once you came to the two knolls, their stone cabin was on the backside of it. Our team was close and we did see the two knolls in the distance. We figured that we got around three miles from the knolls. If you go looking for it, be careful. Most likely you will need a couple of days to explore and scout the backside. Look for any signs of a rock structure. Take your time and plan your trip carefully with transportation, water, food, and emergency equipment. If something happened to you in this area you would be in big trouble.

There is no phone service and no one around for miles to help you. Take a team with you to help scout. This way if there is an emergency, you can depend on others to help. Be safe. The above location and clues (information) have not been released to the public until now. Happy hunting.

Our work wasn't done. We only tried to find another Robbers Roost. The film crew and producers wanted a tv show and we were determined to give them one. They were mainly counting on us to deliver good, solid information and locations. It was time to kick it into gear with our research. From this point forward, we did not go back out in the field. I met with some locals and experts and relayed everything I was learning, including locals of points of interest to the production company. It wasn't until two weeks before we went out to film when I learned who the famous person was that we would be filming with.

I was on the phone with the producer, and they revealed the person's name, Chris Jericho. I still didn't know who that was until the phone call was over and I looked up his name. Chris Jericho the wrestler, I thought to myself. He came with a lot of fans and doing a treasure hunt with him would be great, is what I was told. The day of leaving our homes to arrive in Green River was exciting for our team. We loaded up three vehicles with gear, metal detectors, drones, and other equipment including two large UTVs. When we got to Green River, we stayed at a hotel there and that was our home for the next three days.

We arrived in the evening and were greeted by the producers and filming crew. We all attended a secret meeting in my hotel room and went over the plan. At this point, the only plan was to make a great show and go out and investigate the areas my team was able to research. Later that night, my team and I were quiet in our hotel rooms, charging batteries and prepping for the next day, the first filming day. That morning I met Chris for the first time. He was what I expected him to be. A man with large arms and a stocky body, just like a wrestler. We stood in the hotel hallway for a bit and got acquainted with each other. I learned more about him, and he learned more about my team and I.

Chris Jericho (Left) — Author (Right)

We didn't leave the hotel until around ten o'clock that morning. We learned that the lighting is better later in the day for filming. What we didn't know is how long these filming days were going to be. We headed west on highway 50 for about an hour's drive. There we turned left onto a dirt road and followed it for about thirty minutes. We finally reached the area and vicinity where we were told that Butch Cassidy might have left his name with wagon grease on an overhang. We only had a general idea of where it could be. The biggest clue was the dry river nearby. As soon as we got into the area, filming began and my team did shine. We were all in the frame and the first and most important thing was finding the grease writing.

We loaded up the UVTs and put Chris Jericho and headed down the road with the filming crew. We wanted to let Chris drive so he could have that experience. As we were driving, I kept my eyes out for the dry river bed that matched the description. After about five miles, we found the river and it was just like it was explained to me over the phone. It was to the left of the dirt road with many big round river rocks in the bed. We got out of the vehicles and started scouting. It took some time but one of my guys spotted a cave-like overhang up the river.

The camera crews were not far behind and to our surprise, it was the rock with Butch Cassidy's name on it. The camera crew kept the cameras rolling as Chris and my team admired our discovery.

Even during the cameras on us, I noticed that his name was spelled wrong. I was told it was but I couldn't believe what I was seeing right in front of my eyes. Why would Butch Cassidy spell his name wrong? I went instantly into treasure hunting and deciphering mode. I know in the past, treasure hiders have left clues to confuse others. See from the picture above, it's spelled "Butch Casady" instead of Butch Cassidy. Was he drunk or did someone else write this and didn't know how to spell it correctly? I believe that the writing and wear and tear matched the 1890s. This time, I would call it, seemed off.

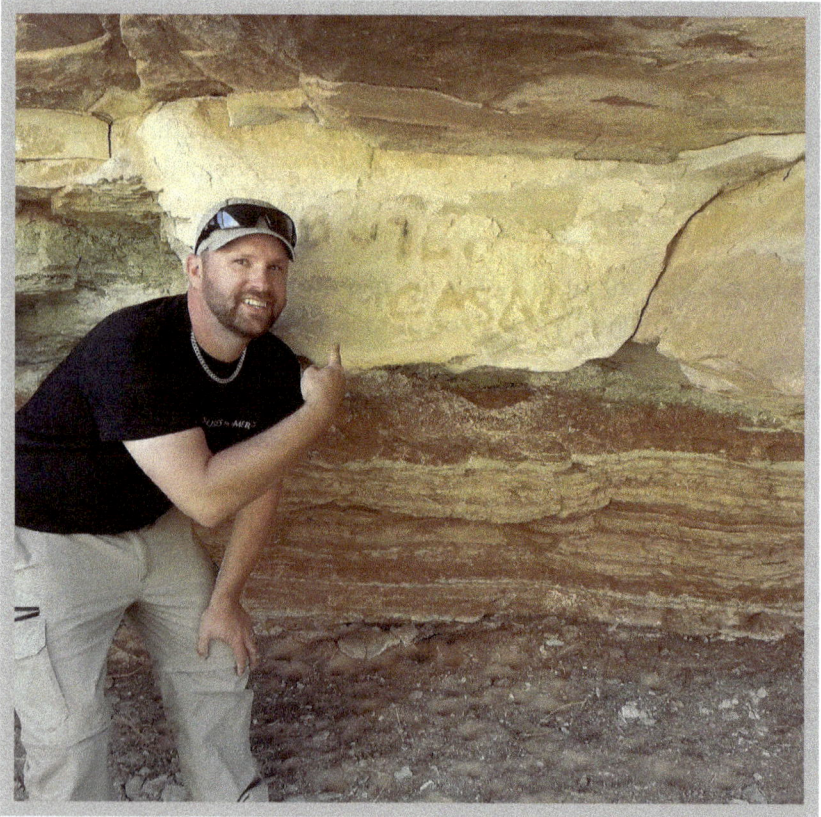

Butch Cassidy Rock of Wagon Grease—Author pictured

I think and I mentioned it on the show, that Butch wrote it this way because he wanted to remember something important when he returned to this area. Its's said that Butch and his gang secretly hid a cache of gold here at this location. If that is true, he would want to purposely spell it wrong to remember that piece of important information. This is not the first and only inscription

Butch has left behind. Tree symbols and rock carvings have been found in the area too, but they were all spelled correctly.

I think there's something to this location. We hunted and scouted that area very well and no hideout or structure was discovered here. Residents and experts said that this was the trail the gang used to get to their hideout. That would be why we didn't find any campsite or cabin in the area. It wasn't a hideout. It was a stopping point or rest area for the Wild Bunch.

We took out our metal detectors and started to scout the area. We did find some old bullets that match the time of the 1880s. These were old bullets and much larger than the commonly used calibers of today's modern guns. By the time we felt that our day was over with investigating the area, it was getting dark. We packed up the UTVs on the trailers and loaded up our gear. The film crew did the same thing, and we were on the highway back to Green River.

By the time we got to the hotel, it was around ten o'clock at night. We were tired and we all went to bed. The next morning, my friend Steve Shaffer and I were asked by Chris Jericho if we would join him on his podcast show, "Talk is Jericho." We happily accepted and went to his hotel room to record. That was a great time to learn more about Chris and his personality. This podcast lasted around an hour and a half. This podcast is on the internet and you can still listen to it. The episode is called "The Real Life Indiana Jones." If you get a chance, you should listen to it because we get into a lot of conversations about treasure hunting and the how-tos.

After the podcast recording was done, we grabbed some breakfast, and once again, my team and the filming crew were on the road again. This time we were searching for the famous Robbers Roost. I was told that if I followed some directions given to me prior to filming, I could find it. This time, we headed south towards Hanksville to locate the hideout. I'm not going to lie, I got the whole crew lost twice, trying to find the area of the hideout. With the clues that were passed to me, I was able to get us close but there were slot canyons everywhere in this area. One wrong turn got us heading in the wrong direction and it took some time and miles to get us back on track.

Not to mention, this is a very remote location still today. When we finally were on the right dirt road, just about ten miles from the vicinity, we were stopped by deep sand dunes blocking the road. At this point, we abandoned the vehicles and unloaded the UTVs. Some of the vehicles couldn't safely get through the dunes without getting stuck in the sand. This caused our first problem of the day because we could only take ten people at a time with the UTVs. Plus we had tons of treasure Hunting equipment and filming equipment to get to the hideout to film. This made this section of the day long and dragged out.

After about three round trips back and forth, we finally had everyone at the mouth of the canyon where I knew we had to start our search. Not just for the hideout, but for an old corral and the buried treasure of gold and silver from the Castle Gate Robbery. While the UTVs were carrying people and equipment back and forth, I started to explore. We found that right where we were unloading the equipment, a very old water well system was built to supply fresh, clean water. This looked like it may have matched the period of Butch Cassidy.

Sand dunes over a dirt road

Once we were ready to film, my team and Chris headed out on foot to explore. We found old inscriptions carved in a rock nearby. Some of them were very old and had dates on them. I learned later that many people in the old days, traveled to this area so they could leave their name, just like Butch Cassidy. We explored that canyon a little more and looked for any clues that could get us closer to finding the gold treasure. Once we realized that the canyon was a dead-end drop, we abandoned that search area. Then from there, we headed back to where we came and decided to follow the deep canyon in the east direction.

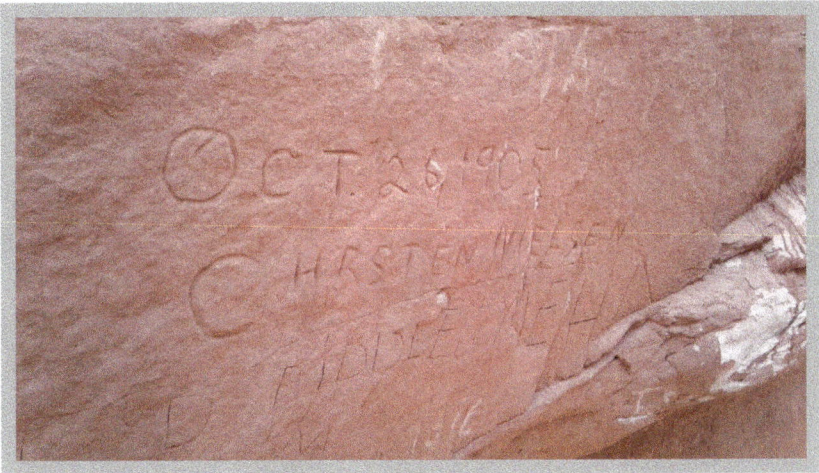

It wasn't more than about a mile in this canyon when Robbers Roost was found. During this time, the Forest Service appointed a representative to come with us, and off camera, he confirmed that the structure we found was in fact the old famous hideout that Butch Cassidy and the Wild Buch used many times to hide from the law. My first impression of the structure is that there wasn't much left. The fireplace and chimney still stand today but the rest of the stone cabin is long gone. If you look close enough, you can still see parts of the footing and the first layer of rock protruding from the ground but that's it. The cameramen were following us around as we inspected the hideout.

Todd got his metal detector out and scouted the area but not much was found in the way of relics and treasure. I'm guessing that this area has been hit by many people before us. This might be why the structure is nearly gone.

In this situation, my team and I knew that we better just leave the ruins alone. We know that if everyone came here and scouted the structure for relics and treasure, it would take much for the rest of the ruins to get destroyed. We decided that we have it on camera, pictures, and memories and we wanted to press on. There were still two more agendas to accomplish.

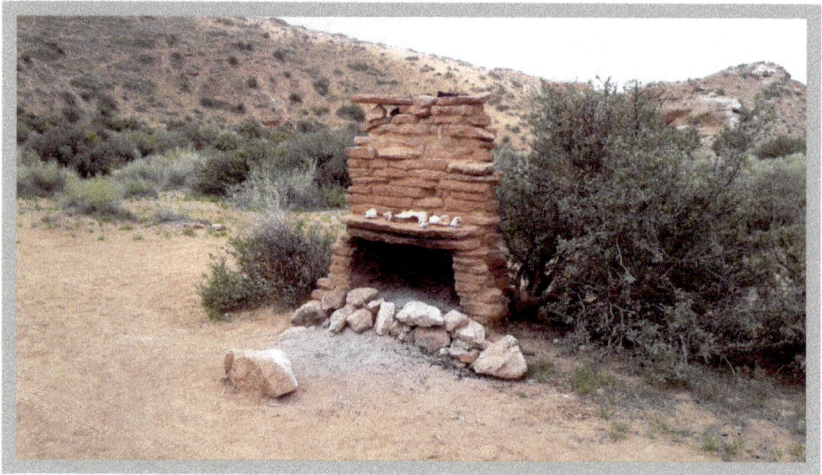

Robbers Roost ruins, Canyonlands, Utah—2017

Finding the lost gold and the old corral used by the Wild Bunch. Just about a half mile to the east of the cabin ruins, we found the old coral, made of old wooden sticks and wire.

Like I mentioned before, Butch was good with horses, and they had many around them at all times. This corral served as a holding place for their horses. We once again took the metal detectors and found an old horseshoe, just outside of it. This was a great find because it's possible that this horseshoe was from one of the horses used by the Wild Bunch.

After investigating the corral inside and out, we decided to split up our team and look for the buried gold. We were looking for any type of clue. Maybe another craving and inscription on a rock. Maybe another structure. We checked all the little side canyons and looked for cave openings.

Robbers Roost horse corral—2017

Todd had his metal detector with him this whole time, trying to find any clues that we could. Unfortunately, we did not find anything else in the area. No clues. No gold. It's very possible that the gold wasn't in the area where we found the hideout. The gang could have stashed it away further into the wilderness. If it was me and I traveled back to this area to look for buried treasure, I would start at this canyon and take my search to the outskirts. The legends say the Castle Gate gold has never been found.

There are no reports of the Wild Bunch or Butch selling or trading the gold. This gang broke up and disappeared shortly after this robbery but reports said that they did stay at Robbers Roost before disappearing forever. Is the gold and treasure in this area still today? I think there's a good possibility of that.

NINE

John Wesley Hardin and the 42 Murders

John Wesley Hardin had many names. He was known as "Little Arkansas", "Wesley Clements", and "J. H. Swain." This outlaw was a bad guy that turned into a lawyer, but we'll get into that later in this chapter. It's possible that John might be one of the most notorious, self-inflicting outlaws of the west. It seems that his own worst enemy was himself. Let me explain and you can make that decision for yourself. In 1853, John was born in Texas, very close to Bonham. His father was James Harden and he was a preacher of the local Christian church. His mother was Elizabeth Dixson and there's not much about her written in history. Nothing that I could find.

John himself was named after the founder of his father's church and some would say, his dad wanted John to live a Christian life. To be faithful to God and to his church. I think it's safe to say that John was raised to have a promising life. His grandfather was a congressman from North Carolina and so was his great-grandfather. But I'm not sure this type of pressure is what John needed. In fact, it may have caused him to rebel in many ways. John's father did travel a lot and did the best he could to teach the word of God and he thrived to be a good missionary. His family relocated to another town in Texas called Sumpter in 1959. During his upcoming, John had nine siblings so this was a full house. John's father became a teacher at the school that his siblings attended.

During school, John was bullied by another student named Charles Sloter. The tension between both of them grew more and more. One day, Charles accused John of writing something inappropriate in the schoolhouse that insulted one of the girls that attended there. The two fourteen-year-old boys argued back and forth until John turned the finger pointing around back at Charles. When that happened, Charles pulled out his pocket knife and charged toward John. John was quick enough to grab Charles's hand and twisted it until the knife stabbed Charles. The whole school witnessed this act and Charles almost died because of it.

Things didn't get any better for John and when he was fifteen years old in 1868, he challenged his uncle's slave to a wrestling match. John won this match, but his troubles were far from over because the next day, his uncle's slave, named Maje, ambushed him. Reports say that John was provoking Maje on the street, waving and yelling. When the chase started, John pulled out his revolver and shot Maje five times. Unfortunately, Maje died three days later due to his wounds. The following is from the account of John himself from a book he wrote, many years later. After the shooting, John's father did not believe his son would be set free because there were many slaves in this area.

He figured that the jury would find John guilty for sure. John's father ordered him to go into hiding but that did not last long. Union soldiers found John's hiding place and tried to arrest him. John wrote that he shot the three soldiers and ran away from the area, knowing that the law would be after him. Some people say that the three soldiers were buried by the townspeople just one hundred yards away from the location where they were murdered. John was on the run because he knew what he did and that he killed four people in such a short amount of time. He was now a known outlaw and murderer and he decided to stay on that path by not turning himself in. Soon after, it's said that he started to ride and travel from town to town with an outlaw named Frank Polk.

Both men were wanted for killing Union soldiers, but Frank was arrested, and John escaped once again. He stayed on the path of least resistance, running and hiding from his troubles. John didn't rest and his murders were coming in quicker than most outlaws of his time. He didn't know how to stay out of trouble, and he was digging his grave faster and faster every time he encountered a person. Doom seemed to surround John and in many ways, it seemed like to enjoyed telling people about his murders and crimes. John became a schoolteacher for a short amount of time, and he caused attention to himself by telling people that he once shot a man in the eye as a bet to win a bottle of whiskey.

He also claimed that he shot more soldiers with his cousin Simp. John just talked about his killings like no one has ever done before. There's more. John was telling everyone that killed a black man just a year or so before becoming a teacher. John gave up teaching and headed out of town and on January 5, 1870, John got into an argument and fought over a deck of cards. Its reported that John was winning at poker, every hand. A man named Benjamin Bradley warned John that he better not win another hand or he would kill him. The fight broke out and John was able to disarm Benjamin. John claims later that night, Benjamin came looking for him and shot at him, missing.

John pulled out his gun and shot Benjamin in the head and in the chest. This caused even more trouble for John because everyone in the area witnessed that shooting. John ran by riding out of town and it wasn't long before a large posse was on his trail, hunting him down. John claimed that he disarmed two members of the posse and took their shotgun and some six-shooters, along with a couple of knives. I couldn't find the records of what happened at that point, but I did find more about the following year. If you thought the killing was done, think again. John continued to live the life of murder, and to make things worse, he bragged about it and even exaggerated his stories.

He became a target for law enforcement and other outlaws. Some outlaws heard about John's stories, and some decided that if they crossed paths with him, they were going to try to make a name for themselves with their six-shooters. In many ways, John had no chance against himself or the people around him. The walls of his life were caving in on him. At this point in John's story, it's hard to say if he lied and stretched the truth of his stories or if he really did kill and murder as many people as he bragged about. Every story he told involved killing, getting arrested, and escaping from the law.

He enjoyed bragging about how good he was with his guns. He told everyone that he was very fast at drawing his six shooters and even explained how he drew his guns. Many gunfighters wanted to cross paths with John to prove if he was as fast as he claimed. According to John and some accounts from others, John met Wild Bill Hickok for the first time in Abilene, Kansas. Wild Bill was the marshal and he was told by townspeople that John was wearing his guns in town. Wild Bill approached John and told him he was there to disarm him.

John did give up his guns, but some would say that John handed them over in an intimidating way. Both barrels pointed right at Wild Bill. This was the end of the event, but some say that Wild Bill and John were seen a couple of months later and they seemed to be in a friendly relationship. Apparently, Wild Bill allowed John to wear his guns in town this time. This was the only story and report I found about wild Bill Hickok and John having anything to do with each other. In 1872, John married Jane Bowen but his crimes and gambling life did not end. In fact, he met up with some of his cousins who had been in the fraud business for several years.

During this time, John once again got in a fight during a poker game and was wounded by a shotgun blast. This is the point in John's life that he thought he wanted to turn himself into the law and end his way of life. He was arrested and taken to jail but shortly after being there, he learned that the sheriff was going to pin many murders on John. After a couple of days, John realized he was going to be sentenced to death, so he managed to escaped from his cell window. During the next year, John traveled to Florida and then back to Texas. He spent some time with other known outlaws, and it seems that he couldn't get away from the life of an outlaw. More fights and shootings happen and his death toll was extremely high at this point.

Even the Governor of Texas put out wanted posters and he was a wanted man for a four-thousand-dollar bounty. In 1877, John was finally arrested and this time was different. The law knew that he was good at escaping and was known for killing officers that have held him captive. They took all the steps they did to keep John in jail until the Judge could sentence him. This trial did not take long and he was sentenced to twenty-five years. The judge threw that book at him and sent him to Huntsville Prison. I can't believe I'm about to tell you this but again, John and other prisoners were caught digging underground tunnels within a few hours of John's arrival.

This wasn't his only time getting caught. For the next couple of years, prison guards found John trying to escape. John just didn't know how to stop. He was truly a bad man that did whatever he wanted and had no remorse. He was relentless. After a couple more years that had gone by, John accepted the prison life that he was forced to serve. At this point, he finally gave up and accepted that he was stuck. He attended school and read many books. He also wrote an autobiography of his life. Then, he got the news that his wife passed away. After seventeen years had gone by, he was released on good behavior and faith that he could be released back into the public.

Believe it or not, he became a law-abiding citizen, and he even passed the bar exam to become a lawyer. John still had a few mishaps and broke that law a few times during gambling and married a young girl too. The marriage didn't last long because John was John. He couldn't help himself and trouble still found him everywhere he went. At this point, I think he knew he couldn't bleed in sociality, and he was finally killed the same way he killed many people before him, death by gun. John had some unfriendly words earlier that day and that same man returned to the saloon and shot John in the back of the head.

He was shot four times total that night. This story struck me as hard to believe. I read many accounts of John Hardin and researched a lot of different stories. He was truly a man that couldn't stay out of trouble. Nor could he walk away from it if it came looking for him. His own decisions and attitude are what led to his death. I'm sure many people could agree that he should have been stopped in his early life. He made my list as one of the roughest and perhaps dumbest outlaws I've ever researched. Writing about his life story painted a good picture for his readers. In total, he claimed that he killed forty-two men.

He literally spells it out in his book and the reader could follow along in his murdering and crime sprees. I do find it ironic that he was shot in the back of the head. According to his life story, he did the same to many others. I guess this is a story about you reap what you sow. John's body resigns in Nixon Texas along with his wife Jane beside him.

TEN

Belle Starr the Female Bandit

Belle Starr, also named the Bandit Queen, was born Myra Belle Shirley in Carthage, Missouri, on February the 5th, 1848. Her parents were John Shirley and Elizabeth Pennington. Her father was known as "the Judge" and known as the trouble-maker of a very highborn, wealthy family name. He supported the Confederates and didn't hide that fact. Her mother was a Hatfield by birth. The same family from the Virginia–Kentucky border town that involved some very interesting history known as the Hatfields and McCoys feud that lasted many, many years. Belle wasn't a child that lived frugally.

Her father was very wealthy and owned a large amount of land and a huge mansion. Shirley seemed to have everything they ever needed. Money, respect, and more. They lived a great life until the Union and the Confederates started to see things differently. In some cases, some would say that Belle had a somewhat spoiled childhood. She had no problem telling everyone who she was and what she thought. She had a promising life. She had musical talent, and she did very well for herself at the girl's academy. She was known to wear very fancy clothes and accessories. Because of her wealthy status, some would say that Belle was very outspoken and confident.

Her brother Bud was known as a gentleman, and he was well respected around town. He was very much like Belle and he had a promising life in front of him. Bud enlisted in the war in the area and learned the manners of battle. When he returned, he spent time teaching Belle how to shoot a gun and to be accurate. Around this time, Bud and Belle were old enough to run and make decisions around the house and for their father's businesses while he was gone. Time was changing in the area. I found some information on Belle in her earlier life, and these are some of the accounts.

Belle married Jim Reed in 1866 at the age of nineteen and gave birth to her first child. Her husband Jim Redd became a salesman. They had another child in 1871. Belle's husband became wanted for killing a man. They decided that moving to California would be a good way to escape the fear of her husband being arrested. This wasn't the first time Belle and her husband were faced with outlaws. Rumor spread that she was seen with a few a couple of years prior. It appeared that Belle had a little bit of a wild side to her and she wasn't afraid to show it from time to time.

After some time in California, the young family relocated to a place called North Canadian River country. Only this time, history may suggest that it wasn't to run, it was to continue that life of unlawful acts. It's said that Belle and Jim joined a gang of outlaws and forced a man to tell them the location of thirty thousand dollars of gold he hit for safekeeping. The gang was successful in finding the gold and once the prize was split, Jim and Belle were on their way back to Texas. It wasn't long until the two were up to their necks in trouble. Belle was said to have ridden her horse, and sidesaddle while shooting her gun.

The black dress she wears feeds into the look and lifestyle of an outlaw. Reed was becoming quite the outlaw himself. He ran around with his gang, committing unlawful acts, robberies, and murders. I think what broke the straws back for Belle is the event that took place in 1874. Her husband's bandit-type ways caught up to him and he was killed. Not only murdered but murdered by one of his own gang members.

This is a time in one's life when you can't depend on or trust anyone. Especially a criminal. Belle was mad and broken-hearted and she left her children with their grandmother. She did this so she didn't worry about her kids. Knowing that they were taken care of, she rode off in the sunset to live a life in Indian Territory. This is where she found herself as a bandit and single woman. It's said that she rode with a few different people, trying to find herself. Believe it or not, she even rode with Jesse James there. She started to fall in love with a Cherokee Indian. This spark turned into love and Belle and Sam Starr were married.

The newlywed couple moved to a sixty-acre property in the Canadian River area. Soon after, Belle and her new lover started a full-blown outlaw outfit and started to do everything they could get away with. Cattle rustling, stealing horses, selling whiskey to Indians. If they could think it, they would do it. The gang started to raise quite a bit of trouble and the leader of the gang was yours truly, Belle Starr. She was behind the plans and ideas. The brains of the group. Belle's gang has been in the works now for about four years and now things were about to go south for them.

Belle and Reed were arrested in 1883 by a man named Bass Reeves. Even though these outlaws have committed many ruthless crimes, they were arrested for horse thieving. Belle was sentenced to nine months in jail and during that time she was there, her husband was killed. He and another gang member crossed paths with a lawman and both were shot and killed. Belle got word of this while she was serving time. Belle returned to her family's home and started her new life again, back where she came from. Things were different than she remembered.

Union soldiers were placed in and around her hometown and she was faced with either changing or being an outcast. The Union had a stronghold around their town and even though Belle's family were considered southerners (Confederates). Belle's father was shot and killed by men who dressed as Yankees. Bud was now forced to run his father's affairs when he returned home. Even though the war was over and the Confederates withdrew, the Yankee presence in the area remained strong and Belle had a new situation on her hands. The Yankees were dividing lands and homes and giving them to the slaves of the area.

These homes and lands were owned by former Confederates. Belle and Bud were forced to live a life in this new world and new ideas, formed by the Yankees (The Union). During this time, Belle was being counted on by a Yankee Major named Thomas Crail. Thomas (Tom) was in charge of the growth of the Union in the area and Belle was a woman that many men sought after. In a nutshell, it seemed that the Yankees won but there were still many confederate loyalists in the South that were going to take to this new life well. This was the beginning of our bitter conflict in this area. Many townspeople fought over both sides of the war. Separating this once peaceful town, things began to start being worse. She met a man named Sam Starr and that's where the trouble began for her. The Union put out the word that if anyone was seen helping a Confederate in any way, they would be arrested and their homes would be burnt and their lands would be taken away.

Sam Starr was a captain of a renegade Confederate group who felt that they were fighting for what they thought was right. Sam rode into town, looking for Belle and he wanted to meet her. Court her if you will. Because this area was pro-Yankee, Belle had to hide her intent and feeling that she was starting to get for Sam. Sam liked to provoke situations, and one night, he met face to face with Major Tom of the Yankees. This was a bold move for Sam and in some ways, you can say that he knew he was causing problems just by showing up at Belle's house that night.

Both men were in charge of their army and Sam's Confederates were hiding out, just a few minutes away from Belle's home. The Yankees were at Belle's home, watching for the Confederates. Sam and his army fled the area but they were chased by Yankees on horses. During the chase, Sam was shot and wounded and fell off his horse. Both armies continued that chase as Sam hid in the cornfield after falling off his horse. He made his way to Belle's house where Bud and she tried to treat Sam's wounds. In a short amount of time, the Yankees returned to Belle's home and discovered that they were helping Sam. Harboring Confederates is a punishable crime and Bud was arrested and their family mansion was burnt to the ground.

This is where Belle had enough. Her father was killed, her brother was placed in jail, and her family's home was gone. She arranged a visit from Major Tom at the jailhouse where Bud and Sam were. Belle had helpers, Sam's men, who busted them out of jail. They were successful and they escaped into the wilderness. They fled to an old cabin deep in the woods. This is where Belle met with Sam's army and they decided that they were going to make a stand. Sam was now a wanted man for murder. Bud wanted his life back and tried to convince Belle that she needed to come back home and face the consequences.

Belle disagreed and told her brother that she would most likely never see him again. She was now on the path of what she felt was right to avenge her family's home and name. Belle and Sam's group was growing larger and larger every day. This group of outlaws was stealing from the Union every chance they got. This group was pushing Union localists out of the state lines. The Union stronghold was not so strong anymore and according to the newspapers, Sam and Belle were taking control of the area. Thieves and outlaws heard a word about the southerners taking over and men were flaking into the area to be recorded by Sam.

Even though Belle thought what they were doing was right, Sam allowed almost everyone with a gun into their group. It grew so large that Sam had to come up with a plan for gaining more money to feed and clothe their men. Without Belle knowing it, Sam ordered his men to rob and steal everything they could get their hands on. What started off as only attacking Union stagecoaches and trains turned into something a lot darker Townspeople's homes, money, and belongings were being taken. Townspeople were being murdered and chaos was on the rise. Unfortunately for Belle, she was face to face with right and wrong.

Sam Starr and Belle Shirley wanted posters and a reward of five thousand dollars was placed all over the state. Belle and Sam fell in love and decided to get married even though the times were dangerous. At this point, Belle became Mrs. Starr and she was sure that they were doing what was right for the south. Later on, in time, her brother Bud came into her camp one day to ask her to come home. The word around the area was that the Union was gaining manpower and their plan was to stop Sam and his group at any cost. Dead or alive, the Union was ready to go to battle to stop the crimes. Bud told Belle that if she gave herself up at this time, Major Tom would let her off easy for her crimes.

Bud was hoping that Belle could turn her life around. Bud told Belle that her group of outlaws was not just hurting and stealing from the Union but they were hurting innocent people and businesses. Bud explained that the state of Missouri was cracking down on their group and that she would be killed if she didn't stop. Belle was shocked to find out that Sam has been ordering these vicious crimes against the south. She wasn't aware that their men were doing this. She thought they were still attacking Union money and supplies. When Bud rode out of Belle's camp, he was mistaken for a Union trespasser and one of the outlaws shot him.

Belle ran to Bud and he died in her arms at that moment. Belle had a change of heart because of her brother's death and what he told her. She confronted Sam and he did not deny what Bud was saying. Belle did not agree with Sam and she gave him her wedding ring back and left camp. Her upbringing did not permit this type of behavior and even though she loved Sam, she had to leave. She felt that the cause that moved into the typical outlaw ways was now lost. This group was nothing but bandits at this point in her opinion. Belle was staying at a homestead that was friendly to her and her family and they kept her hidden for a time.

Belle and Sam wanted posters moved to a higher reward price of ten thousand dollars and many people were out to collect the reward. This was a huge reward and many people wanted to take advantage of that kind of money. Plus, Belle, Sam, and their men had been causing a lot of trouble in the area. I believe many people wanted the fighting, robberies, and killing to come to an end. That was an extremely large amount of money back in those days.

Meanwhile, Major Tom's men were ready for war. The Union had many troops ready for Sam and his men in town. One night, Belle was told that Sam and his men were going to be ambushed and she wasted no time and jumped on her horse to ride off to find Sam. Even though she disagreed with him, he was her husband and she wanted to save him because she loved him. As she was riding in the darkness of the night, Sam and his bandits were riding towards the town and Tom's Yankees were waiting in town for Sam. Belle had no idea what was about to happen.

All she knew was that her love was going to be ambushed and killed. During this event, a local townsman followed a friend of Belle's and discovered that she was going to ride out to stop Sam. He decided to ride ahead of her and found a spot on the road where he could hide in the thick trees, just off the road a bit. He was sitting down with a shotgun and waiting for Belle, hiding in the darkness. When Belle rode towards him, he waited for the right shot. He shot her once and she fell off her horse. He walked up to her and shot her again to make sure she was dead. Belle was forty-one years old when she was shot.

The man that collected the reward was not invited in a friendly way to town afterward. Belle and her family's name was still intact when it came down to how the townspeople thought about her. Soon after, Sam rode into town to surrender himself. The townspeople and Union soldiers watched him ride calmly down the main street and watched him walk into Major Toms office building. Both men cared for Belle and didn't want her to die. The fact of the matter is, that both men were soldiers and they respected the law of war. Sam gave himself up in a peaceful way and Tom also showed that same respect for him.

Tom allowed Sam to see Belle's body and they claimed that the dead woman in front of them was not Belle Starr. The man who shot her and wanted to collect the money was mad because Major Tom refused to give him the money for her death. Even though it was Belle, Tom and Sam didn't feel that a coward should collect so much money by shooting a female. A respected female. Love and human behaviors are strange things and always have been. Belle is still remembered today as a female icon. Her integrity and spirit were kept intact due to the men that loved her. This story goes to show that not all outlaws are what we think of them today.

Times were different and many people reacted in different ways than we do today. Belles story was told around this area for many years to come. Even though the Union and Confederates thought differently and were on completely different sides of the political sector, Belles story still lives on. This was one account but many people believe that Belle was never shot and that she lived her life in a faraway place even after Sam was killed in a gunfight on December 17, 1886. Some say that Belle's story lived on and she continued her way of life. I'll leave this part to you to ponder on and look into yourself.

ELEVEN

Bill Doolin Founder of the Doolin-Dalton Gang

William Doolin, also known as Bill or Will Barry was an outlaw in the old western days that founded the notorious Doolin-Dalton Gang from Oklahoma. His gang was also called the Wild Bunch and or the Oklahombres gang. This group of outlaws was into the organized robbing of banks, trains, and stagecoaches. Oklahoma was a free, open range state where brave cowboys and cattlemen could go out and stake their own land. Through hard work, a man could make a good life and raise cattle. That only lasted for so long until the state started to cut off the ranchers by dividing and separating the land with wire fences, claiming what land it wanted.

Only giving to who and what it wanted. This ended much of the private independent ranchers. This started a feud between many cowboys and ranchers and some decided to pick up their guns instead of sitting back and accepting the new way. One by one gangs and outlaws fought with anger to claim what they thought was rightfully theirs. Marshals were hired to take control of the area. As the marshals tried to stop the robbing and looting another gang was formed. The gang that really made a difference for the right or wrong reasoning was the Doolin Gang. This is their story and it begins in the mid-1800s.

Let's move forward to 1858 when William Doolin was born in Johnson County Arkansas. Because his family didn't come from money and his dad wasn't a governor, judge, or something along those lines, there's not much about his childhood. His father was named Michael Doolin and he was born in Logan Kentuck in 1808. His parents were John Doolin and Cathy Rowe. Bill's father was married twice in his life and he died in 1865. His biological mother was named Artemina (Bellar) Dollin and she married Michael when she was thirty-six years old. After the death of his father, Bill, his mother ran their family's farm for many years.

When Bill was a young adult, his mother moved to Fort Smith and sold the family farm. Bill had one brother named Tennessee Dollin who was born in 1862. This family was soon separated because Bill's brother and mother moved away and he left Arkansas to relocate to Oklahoma when he was twenty-three years old. This area was known as Indian territory and it was a promising place for ranchers and cattlemen. Bill continued to work as a ranch hand for several employers. After some time he became friends with the Dalton family. The Dalton family was known as a group of renegades that rebelled against the land closure by the state.

When the land wasn't free for the taking, the Dalton Gang was formed and they started to rob banks in the area. They claimed that they stood for the common folk in Oklahoma. They lived in the state of mind that if their lands could be taken away, making them lose their livelihood, they should and would rob back what was theirs. Bill was somewhat more on the good side of these outlaw activities at first. He was involved with a few bank robberies but he wasn't seen by the locals as the main threat. He was able to slip through the cracks enough to where he wasn't a wanted man at this time.

He was seen as more of an employee. It didn't take long for the Dalton Gang to make a name for themselves. Robbing local businesses and banks was something they did on a frequent basis. The Dalton Gang wasn't the only group of outlaws that decided they would take what they wanted in the area. Three other gangs were in Oklahoma doing the same thing. Living a life of robbing and thieving. The Dalton gang became quite bold and started robbing even more and more as time went by. The law couldn't keep up with all the crime which allowed them to be more successful in the county. Not to mention that other common folks were not opposed to their criminal activities.

Some of the townspeople believed that these gangs were teaching the government a lesson and they too felt like their lands being taken were an act of piracy. This made the situation worse and a little more complicated. It wasn't the typical manner of the townspeople looking out for the law. Not many people were turning in information and the whereabouts of the gang's locations and criminal activities. Not everyone felt this way. The law was getting stronger and stronger in the area. Due to the robberies, the local marshals were granted permission to deputize more recruits.

Now that the law had more help, they started to become more proactive. They started to get one step ahead of these gangs and started to crack down on them. The Dalton Gang came to an end one day when they decided to rob two banks in town at the same time. The law was waiting for them and had plenty of guns ready. As the Dalton gang walked out of the banks, holding bags of money, the law started to fire their guns. The Dalton Gang was taken by surprise and every one of them that was involved with this robbery was shot and killed. This was a victory for the law. At this point in time, the outlaw gangs were stopped. Some of the townspeople felt that the territory would settle down, but there was one man they overlooked.

Bill came into town a couple of days after the Dalton gang was killed. He tried to stay out of sight because the rest of the Dalton gang was being hunted down. Bill was placed in a situation where he found a wounded Dalton member and tried to help him in a nearby stable. Because of the reward and wanted posters placed around town, some people wanted to collect their money by finding Dalton members. As Bill was helping his wounded friend, a man shot him in the head and the town was alerted by the gunshots. Bill then in return shot the man that killed his friend, and that's when Bill's life changed forever.

Townspeople were yelling in the streets, "Dalton Member. Daltons are here!" That caused Bill to remain hidden in the shadows of the night and he made his way out of town. Now Bill was wanted for murder. Some felt that it was self-defense but nevertheless, he was a wanted man and doomed as an outlaw. Bill spent the next few months hiding and staying out of the town's limits. He stayed in hiding and slept under the stars for months. He was alone. No one to talk with and he didn't dare to show his face in any town. Because he was an outcast and branded a murderer, he found that the only companionship he could associate with was with other outlaws. He was on the run and he needed to come up with a plan to live a life once again.

Bill was now becoming friends with other outcasts and outlaws that were also hiding from the law. This is a situation much like modern-day criminals. If these types of people are in hiding with nothing to do, they can and will resort to more crime. Bill became well known in this group of men and he was a thinker. He was coming up with ideas of what this group could do and how they could make a better living for themselves. Bill soon was looked at as a leader of the group. They knew he was friends and acted on criminal activities with the Dalton gang. He made a good natural leader for this group and soon, they returned to the life of crime.

Now that Bill was the leader, he decided that they needed more men. He knew that they would be more successful with a larger gang. He and his men started riding out in the country again, recruiting other outlaws. This was the start of the Doolin Gang of Oklahoma. Because his gang became large, they started to ride into towns once again. The longer they stayed together as a group of outlaws, the more confident their gang became. Staying at hotels and eating at restaurants, the gang became more known in the area. They were not hiding any longer and this life was much better than they were living in the prior months. Bill was very good at organizing bank robberies. The Doolin Gang would ride into a new town and stake the area out for days and even weeks.

They would appear in public as doing nothing wrong but in reality, they were observing and planning their next moves. As I mentioned earlier, not all the Oklahoma people thought of the Doolin Gang members as bad people. In fact, some townspeople started to inform Bill and his gang of schedules of stagecoaches, bank transfers, and when local law enforcement was occupied on other matters. This made it easier for Bill and his men to stay ahead of the law. They had inside information that made robberies go along more successfully. While the gang was staking out the towns, they mostly stayed out of trouble. This made even better relations between them and the townspeople.

Bill and his gang even busted other outlaws out of jail. Not in the way you would think. Guns blazing. They were more subtle and frugal about it. Because of this well-mannered outlaw personality, Bill was successful in gaining even more outlaws on his side. Bill had everything right where he wanted it. For a known outlaw life, the Doolins Gang had it pretty good. The gang consisted of many men, and some were known as:

- William Marion "Bill" Dalton.
- George "Bitter Creek" Newcomb.
- Charley Pierce.
- Oliver "Ol" Yantis.
- William "Tulsa Jack" Blake.
- Dan "Dynamite Dick" Clifton.
- Roy Daugherty "Arkansas Tom Jones"
- Bill Doolin himself

All these men were known for their talents with a six-shooter and outlaw manners. The gang was on the run, but this time it was different. They were successfully robbing banks and making some good money. The Doolin Gang was able to per-sway bank tellers and vault key holders in a way of not shooting and killing but intimidating. This kept the death toll and murders down low. This wasn't the normal outlaw gang that came into town, shooting and killing people. No Bill and his gang were more on the refined side of the outlaw life. Bill used his smarts again and when the heat was turned up on his gang, he would pay them off with the proceeds of their robberies and split them up from time to time.

Bill would tell his gang members to take their money and go out of the state for a while. His gang members would ride off the state and some would head west while others would head east. This made it very hard for the law to track them down. Sometimes, the Doolin Gang was nowhere to be found for months and months. When they did show up again, it would be in a new territory of Oklahoma and a different town. Bill was known to have compassion for his members. Some would say that he would put himself in harm's way before he would let one of his members go down. Here's an example. After one of their bank robberies, the law tracked them down at an inn outside of town.

The Doolin Gang rode out of the Inn and Bill stayed alongside his men and they rode off, one by one as the posse was hot on their trail. Bill signaled to one member at a time while running with their horses on the trail into the wilderness. One by one gang members would veer off the road, hiding behind natural rock formations and clustered trees. When the posse passed one of the hiding gang members, he would ride off in the other direction. This made it hard for the posse to track them on the road. The Doolin gang got away with this attempt for freedom. Bill and his gang members were now split up over the next few months and they all awaited word from Bill. They stayed in hiding until further notice from their leader.

During this time, Bill stayed in the state and surrounding territory of Oklahoma. He tried to stay hidden and go unnoticed but sometimes, he found himself running from the law. As time went by, Bill found himself living a lonely life once again. He was on the run but one day, he met someone that would change the way Bill operated. During one of his town visits, Bill met a woman named Edith Ellsworth. She wasn't aware of Bill's past outlaw life and he didn't tell her. He even used a fake name so his identity could remain secret and unknown. The heart would not permit Bill to leave the area where Edith lived.

Bill even bought a spread of land outside of her town and played the role of a normal life. He courted her for some time and they started to fall in love. Some say that Edith learned that her new lover was the known outlaw Bill Doolin and some say that she was unaware of his past life. That is something that I could confirm or deny while researching this story. But nevertheless, they got married in Kingfisher Oklahoma and had a son named Jay. Bill's old life came back looking for him once the gang started committing crimes again. Robbing trains and banks. His Doolin gang was back in Oklahoma and they were looking for Bill. Now there are two sides to this story that I discovered.

The first account claims that Edith didn't know about Bill's outlaw past life and a few years later when she found out, she left Bill. In this story, Edith stayed away from Bill and remarried a man named Samuel M. Meek. and lived out her new life. The second account tells a slightly different story that she stayed with Bill and remarried a few years later but met with Bill from time to time in secret. I can't find real evidence that supports either story but one thing is a fact, she did marry another man and Bill re-entered the life of an outlaw, even stronger and more misguided than ever.

I believe there might have been some secret meeting places for Bill and Edith for a couple of years but that stopped when she remarried. I'm guessing she came to the terms that Bill and she would not be able to stay together and she needed to start a new life. But the thing is, she never left their home. She stayed at their homestead and history shows that Bill stayed away to protect her. Bill and his Doolin gang were back at it again. Robbing trains were now on their radar. They would just rob the safes on the trains, they robbed passengers, too.

When the gang would stop the trains, they broke into the vaults and safes while other gang members would walk through the train cars with bags and tell the passengers to take the contents out of their pockets and put them in the bags. After many successful robberies, the law was once again after the Doolin gang. The once quiet and somewhat peaceful gang was not so quiet anymore. Bill had bigger and better plans to make money faster. Soon many law enforcement officials were after the gang and tracking their behavior was something they learned to do. The Doolin gang still remains to save their faces with some local townspeople.

Some localists help protect and hide the Doolin gang from the law. Not only were Bill and his gang not considered vicious murderers, but they also spent a lot of their money at saloons and hotels. This helps their reputation in the state of Oklahoma and to put it frankly, some Oklahoma people still remain bitter towards the government of their state. Times were different these days and some outlaws were angry killers, hurting people everywhere they went. The Doolin Gang didn't conduct their activities this way. The gang was in need of a few things and women were one of those.

Some of the Doolin members were starting to fall for local girls in one area in particular and that started to change the way the gang functioned. Ingalls Oklahoma was a place that the Doolin gang would not rob or steal from. It's believed that this town was where the gang came to meet their lady friends and spent a lot of money. It took the law and government officials one year to map the gang's activities and notice that this town was a haven for the gang. The Doolin gang continued as they always did, robbing more and more banks. The Doolin gang was really doing very well for themselves, and money was not an issue.

The biggest issue was the law, and it was cracking down harder and harder on them. Bill had to change some of his plans and techniques when it came to robbing. Some would say that the Doolin Gang should have stopped while they were ahead but they didn't. This would be the death of the gang as history knew it. Bill was not himself. As the law weighed heavy on his mind, some say so did his broken heart.

The gang noticed some reckless patterns that occurred in Bill's behavior. Bill allowed a couple of female outlaws to start running with them.

Cattle Annie and Little Britches were known as some of the most famous female outlaws in the west. Both were cattle rustlers in Oklahoma and they were known to work alongside the Doolin gang from time to time. These female outlaws may not be mentioned as often as they should in history. Little Britches' real name was Jennie Stevens and Cattle Annie was Ana McDoulet. Both girls were very well known for their skills with a six-shooter and some would compare them to the famously well-known Belle Starr. The Doolin Gang found themselves surrounded by the law in town. Gunfire could be heard throughout the whole town. The law was right this time and they ambushed the gang in Ingalls Oklahoma. This is remembered as the Battle of Ingalls.

After some fighting and many gunshots, the Doolin Gang managed to escape from this large posse. Cattle Annie was with the gang during this gunfight but the gang left her behind. Some of the gang members were wounded during this escape. Tom Jones of the Doolin Gang was arrested during this ambush and Bill knew that it was only a matter of time until the rest of the gang was arrested. The posse did not give up. They followed the gang to a homestead just out of town. The Doolin gang made a great escape once again and now they were on the run. Much like the run they had back in their earlier days. Camping under the stars and staying out of sight. They stayed away from the towns of Oklahoma and continued to hide in the wilderness.

At this point, some of the gang spit up once again. Some of them continued the life of an outlaw but Bill tried to blend in and use a different name to hide his identity once again. In 1895, Charlie Pierce and George "Bitter Creek" were killed after robbing a train. The law was able to track their trail and when they caught up to the two outlaws, they were shot and laid dead on the ground. From this point on, the Doolin Gang members were hunted and killed one after another. During this time, Bill decided to get into the cattle business one day by rustling a large herd up.

He was on the outskirts of town when he was told that the law found where he was hiding and they planned on arresting him. "Little Dick and Bill fled to New Mexico to get away from the law, hopefully for good. Once Bill had time to think about his new place of living, he decided to surrender and negotiate for a smaller sentence for his life of crime. He was rejected many times. Little Bill was captured and arrested. He was wounded by gunshots and died in prison after his sentence. Bill moved to Eureka Springs and he did have Edith with him. She never left and he was tired of living away from her. They lived together once again and the two tried to stay out of the way of the law. Bill wasn't the same man anymore. He had been wounded in the foot from a gunshot during one of his escapes.

Bill and Edith were laying low and were able to stay free for a little longer until Bill Tilghman came into the picture. He was a known lawman that spent a lot of time and effort tracking down Bill's whereabouts. In 1896, Tilghman single-handedly pulled Bill aside while he and Edith were staying at a resort. Even though Bill was jailed, it didn't stop him. Even though some of his gang members were dead, many were still in the area and heard of Bill's capture.

A total of thirteen outlaws rode out to the jail where Bill was detained, and they managed to help him escape once again. They fled, and the last place that Bill and Edith were reported was in Lawson, Oklahoma.

The law tracked him down very quickly and once they had him and his wife surrounded, Bill did not try to back down this time. Nor did he escape. Bill was faced by a man named Marsal Heck Thomas, holding a shotgun, pointed right at him. When Bill refused to come quietly, the marshal shot and killed Bill. At the time of Bill's death, he was placed out in the public on display. This is something that was commonly done when a known outlaw was shot and killed by the law. In some ways, it tells the townspeople that the trouble is gone, and it also shows that crime doesn't pay in the end.

His picture was taken and sold for twenty-five cents. Bill's body was buried at the boot hill of Summit View Cemetery in Guthrie Oklahoma. Later, after Bill's death, Edith filed a lawsuit against the marshal that killed him. She tried to sue for fifty-thousand dollars for the unlawful arrest and shooting but that case was rejected by the court. She later married Samuel M. Meek on February 14th, 1897. She lived until the age of fifty-seven and died in Ponca City, Oklahoma, on September 22nd, 1928. All the original members of the Doolin Gang were killed soon after Bill died.

Some of the newer gang members stopped their Doolin Gang activities and went on with their lives. The Dalton-Doolin Gang is still very well-known in history. This once lawless and outlaw living area now rests and is intertwined into the modern way of living, just like the rest of the United States.

TWELVE

Sam Bass the Train Robber

Sam Bass was a famous outlaw, leader, and notorious train robber. He was known for founding and operating two different groups of gangs in his life. The Black Hills Bandits of Deadwood, South Dakota in 1876 - 1877 and the Bass Gang of Texas in 1877 - 1878. Sam was deeply rooted in the outlaw life and ran with some of the most famously known outlaws. To understand Sam's story, I'm going to start from the beginning and go from there. This is his story and it doesn't just belong to him. I'll talk about many events and people in this chapter.

On July 21st, 1851, Sam was born in Mitchell Indiana. His parents were Daniel Bass and Elizabeth Jane Bass. His father was born on May 3rd of 1821 in North Carolina. He was married twice in his life. He died at the age of forty-two years old on February 20th, 1864. He was buried at the Sheeks Cemetery in Bedford Lawrence, Indiana. Sam was only thirteen years old when his father died. In those days, it was hard to lose the man of the house. Daniel fathered seven children and that made it even hard for Sam's mom. Elizabeth Jane was born on December 17th, 1821 in Lawrence County Indiana. She married Sam's father on October 20th, 1840 at the age of nineteen years old.

She lost two of her children at young ages, leaving her with five in total. She died June 3rd, 1861 at the age of thirty-nine years old. She died just a few short years after Sam left home. Sam was parentless at a young age. He was young when he was orphaned to his uncle and then given to Sherriff Everhart. The Sheriff employed him and took him to Texas. In a way, Everhart raised him and showed him the ways of a man during those times. Overall, Sam was a good young man and lived a pretty normal life. He loved horses and even got into horse racing by purchasing his own to enter in the local races. Even though Sam enjoyed this very much, he still had to work.

After a few years, Sam was a man to make his own choices and he left Denton County in 1877. He learned a great deal about being a cattleman from Everhart and he used those abilities to land him more jobs like that in the time to come. He relocated to San Antonio Texas and worked a few jobs as a cattle hand. Making ends meet, Sam still lived a quiet life in his new area. One day, Sam was told that a successful cattleman named Joel Collins was planning on driving a huge herd of cattle North. Sam heard of this new job opportunity and took it. He figured that money would be good and the new lands and opportunities would be exciting for him. Little did he know that his life was about to change forever because of this decision.

For six months Sam lived the life of a cowboy. Sleeping under the stars and long days of following and directing the herd to Deadwood townsite. The days were long but a meal was available and ready to eat every morning and night. During this time, Sam got to know the other cowboys he was riding with. By the time the herd arrived safely in Deadwood, his employer wasted no time paying Sam. He had money in his pocket and during those times, six months of pay was quite a bit of change. Deadwood was a very thriving mining town and it developed from a miner's camp to a booming town made of wooden buildings.

Deadwood was not a stranger to new people coming and going every day. Famously known people would come to it just to see what all the talk was about. There were hotels, saloons, gambling tables, and of course girls for every man seeking temporary love. This town was growing fast. The money that was made from its gold and silver shined and polished its streets. Sam was a young man in a very popular place. This was a place to admire and a place to fear. Much of the old western history is untamed itself and I had to really dig deep to see what happened to Sam during his time in Deadwood.

There are two different stories that seem to hold water in my option. (Story One) The first After Sam was paid by Joel Collins, he owed his partners and creditors in Texas a big proportion of the money received for the cattle. After Joel paid off his cowboys, he decided to stay in town for a while and try his hand at gambling. He was smitten with the possibility of striking it rich in the saloons but after some time, he was losing his money and wasn't winning it back. Joel was now gambling with all his money, trying to win it back. More and more money was lost and soon he came to realize that he would not be able to pay back his partners and banks to whom he owed money.

Instead of facing the facts and trying to fix the problem, he continued to gamble until it was all gone. Joel couldn't go back to Texas without the money he owed so he met up with some of the cowboys he hired to herd his cattle and had a new proposition for them. Sam was included in this meeting. Joel asked these cowboys if they would come with him on a robbing spree and earn money by robbing the stagecoaches coming into Deadwood. Sam and the other cowboys accepted the terms and that's when the Black Hills Bandits outlaw gang was born. They robbed their way right out of town.

Making money and stealing the gold and silver, including paper money coming and going from the banks on these stagecoaches. (Story Two) When Sam got to Deadwood he was paid by Joel and he spent some time living there and admiring the growth of this booming town. He and his employer Joel decided that they wanted to try their luck at mining. The gold fever got into their veins and they wanted to see if they could strike it rich. Joel and Sam both failed at mining and after investing all their money into a claim, Joel couldn't face his partners and creditors back in Texas. Joel and Sam decided that they would rob stagecoaches to earn their money back.

Either story is good and I'm not sure if it matters so much if it was gambling or the failed gold mine that led to their financial losses. The fact of the matter is that Joel and Sam decided that the outlaw life was far better than not. The Black Hills Bandits was formed and it consisted of many men. Some of their names were:

- Tom Nixon
- Bill Heffridge
- Jack Davis
- Jim Berry
- Joel Collins
- Sam Bass

All these men became the gang of Deadwood and started to make the wrong name for themselves. One of the stagecoach robberies went wrong; the driver named Johnny Slaughter was shot and killed by the Bandit group. Some say Calamity Jane saw the horses from the stagecoach, running through town and she stopped them from tearing up the streets.

The gunshot from the Black Hills Bandits that killed the driver, scared the stagecoach horses and sent them running. After some time, the outlaw gang did some math and decided that the robbing of stagecoaches didn't make enough money to satisfy their hunger for money. The gang decided to move on to bigger and better things. Sam and his gang wanted more than what they were getting at Deadwood. In a place like Deadwood, they couldn't go too far in their criminal activities because it was a rough town as it was. In a place like that, there's always a bigger fish.

The bandits were next seen in Big Springs Nebraska. This was a much easier place to live and to blend in as long as the gang didn't cause too much attention to themselves. Sam organized a plan to rob their first train. The preparation was set in motion and the outlaws were getting ready for a big score. The outlaws first took over the train station and its master by force. It wasn't long until some members of the gang destroyed the telegraph so the train and its company had no communication with each other.

The date was September 18th, 1877 and the people involved

never forgot that day. At 10;48 PM, the train master was ordered by the Black Hills Bandits to signal the train to stop. Once it came to a halt, six members of the gang boarded it. In the first act of this robbery, the bandits were starting to doubt Sam's ability to research what items were aboard a train. Only four hundred and fifty dollars was found in the safe. This save was supposed to be loaded with money. Enough money the bandits could make off into the sunset and never look back. An argument broke out among the outlaws and Sam was convinced that more could be found. He told his group to keep searching for the train cars.

The outlaw team was lucky that day because an unscheduled load was aboard the train. They found wooden boxes and they wasted no time breaking them open. Once all the boxes were opened, they discovered that they found over sixty-thousand dollars' worth of brand new minted gold coins. Each gold coin was a twenty dollar piece coin. The outlaws weren't done with this train yet. Out of greed, they decided to rob the passengers too. One by one, each person was ordered to empty their pockets. The bandits placed all the valuables into bags. They found several gold watches and another fifteen hundred dollars on these passengers.

This was a huge job for the Black Hills Bandits. No one that heard of the robbery in person or in newspapers thought these bandits were anything but successful outlaws. The robbery made headlines for weeks to come. Many newspapers in many different states were talking about this train robbery. It was one of the most famously known. After the robbery, the Blank Hills Bandits split their profits and headed in different directions. Bystanders did describe the outlaw's appearances and the Black Hills gang was on the run. Every lawman in the area was looking for the gang. It wasn't long until the law was hot on their trail. Joel Collins and his partners were shot and killed just a few days after the robbery.

James Berry was captured and arrested for his crimes. This was pretty much the end of his career and the end of his story and history. He wasn't reported about much after that. Many people assume that Nixon had to escape the arrest. He was last seen with Berry, but he wasn't arrested. Many people think he took his share that was split in six ways and made his way to Canada to leave the life of a bandit for good. Sam and Jack Davis both left together and made their way back to Texas. Sam is a smart person because on their way to Texas, soldiers connected with him and he convinced them that they too were looking for the bandits that robbed the train.

I'm sure Sam and Jack were scared at this moment. The soldiers were deployed to track down the bandits and arrest them. The life of the robber was not over for Sam, even though some of his gang members were arrested and killed. After he arrived in Texas, he started mingling with other outlaws. During this time, Sam was getting more and more comfortable talking about his train robberies to these other bandits. After some time of them hearing about how much money he made, they started talking about forming a new gang and working together in the Texas area.

This was the beginning of the "Sam Bass Gang". This new gang started to hit and rob trains for the first time working together. These robberies did not provide the type of money that Sam made from his first robbery. In fact, people started to wonder if Sam hid his money and gold in a cave near Denton Texas. He wasn't seen with a lot of money on him at one time while visiting towns. This might be some-thing for you to consider if you live in the area of Denton. A possible treasure of hidden gold stashed away in a cave for safekeeping. We'll get more into treasures later in this book.

The Sam Bass Gang held up several more trains but their payout was more in the twelve hundred mark and the money wasn't all that good. It almost seemed that the gang was getting hungry for a big job. Something that would payout a lot more money than they have been getting. Living the life of an outlaw is hard on the run and if the money isn't good, it makes them question why they are living the lifestyle. But as wanted men, they couldn't just stop. They needed a lot of money to disappear for even.

Texas Rangers were becoming stronger than ever and they were cracking down on all bandits and outlaws that broke the law. This era is known as the "Bass War". Sam and his gang had the Texas Rangers running around, trying to capture and stop the robberies. This war lasted around four months. As the Rangers were chasing the gang, more and more crimes were committed. Outlaws and bandits started to come out of the tool shed and they too committed many crimes. This led up to a lot of problems and trouble for the state of Texas.

Texas Rangers was desperate and they started to raid and investigate all Texas residences. If they heard that you may have harbored an outlaw or Sam's gang, they rode out to that homestead to inquire about it. Jim Murphy and his father were arrested for working with the Sam Gang and they were faced with their punishments. They were given a choice, go to prison or help us capture and stop the Sam Gang. Jim expected the task and he was released to rejoin the gang and Sam. From this point, there were many failed attempts to capture the gang. There were events where Sam and his outlaws did get into gunfights with the Texas Rangers, but Sam always seemed to get away.

Sam was shot twice but one bullet hit his rifle and one hit his metal belt. Both shots were close but he was able to ride off without any injuries. Not all of the gang were as lucky as Sam. Later Arkansas Johnson was killed by the law and Henry Underwood rode off and he was never heard from again. The gang had no idea where he was. He was just gone and history does not speak of him after that. The Bass Gang was riding out to the Round Rock area one day and Jim Murphy, the one that's now working with the Rangers, was able to slip away for some time to send a letter to Major Jones, explaining the gangs' plans and whereabouts.

Sam and his group were planning on robbing a bank that was in the vicinity of the Round Rock area. The Major prepared his Rangers to travel south to ambush the gang and to stop them from further crimes. A man was placed on the main route, in and out of Round Rock and the Sam Gang was spotted. This lookout rode back into town and told the sheriff what and who he saw. At this point, the law was ready to take down the gang members. They bunkered in town to wait to see if the gang would show themselves. One of the lawmen did in fact see some of the gang members in town. He walked right past a few of them as the gang was watching the bank from the outside.

He followed the outlaws to a tobacco store and came up right behind Sam and asked him if he was wearing a gun. Sam replied "Yes, and I'll let you have it." Sam's gang opened fire immediately and killed the lawman named Grimes. The lawman had no time to react and he was found dead on the ground with six bullet holes in his body. Once the gunfire started, more lawmen came into the building, shooting anyone that stood by Sam. One of the bullets did hit Sam and it went right through his hand, wounding him. Then another shoot went off and that bullet hit Sam right in his chest. By this time, every lawman in town was running down the streets, holding their guns, ready for a fight.

As some of the outlaws were riding out of town, another lawman was spotted by them, running to the communication building to contact more reinforcements. Major Jones open-fired at the run-away outlaws and they returned fire, turning from their horse backward and shooting at the Major. He was lucky that day because one of the bullets just missed him and hit the building next to him. Even though the gang was riding out of town, one lone, unnamed lawman, picked up Grime's gun laying on the floor and started shooting at the outlaws. The outlaws were all mounted on their horses but that didn't stop the lawmen from taking aim with their long rifles. Bullets shooting there and bullets shooting there, over and over again, making a sight to be seen.

Reports say that Jim Murphy stayed in town because, at this point, he was afraid Sam would know that he was the one that tipped off the law. He said that he was watching Sam and Frank leaving town on Frank's horse. Sam was wounded badly and Frank had to lay Sam over his horse to make a clean getaway. Now the law knew Sam was wounded badly and they wasted no time going after them. A posse was formed and they rode out to where the Sam Gang camp was. When they got there, they found nothing. Sam and his gang packed up their things and left. Tracks were spotted leaving the campsite and they led into the trees and wilderness.

During this ride, Sam convinced Frank to leave him. Sam was in too much pain to continue the ride out of the area. Frank did leave Sam but left him a horse and saddle so if Sam survived, he could make it out of the area. Some time went by and the gang was not pursued any further at this time. The law knew that Sam was hurt badly and that only four gang members were left alive. That did not mean that they weren't going to ride out to find them. They just stopped to regroup back in town to come up with a new plan. The next day, Sam was found propped up against a tree where Frank left him. As the law approached him, a voice said, "I'm Sam Bass. The man you are looking for."

The lawmen walked up to the bloody site of Sam and gave him some water, and put him on a wagon, riding back to Round Rock. It was obvious that Sam was dying of his wounds. He was placed in a shack in town while the officials of the court were contacted. Sam heard that he killed a man, escaping out of town and he replied with a comment that many would not expect. He claimed that he was sorry if he did indeed kill a man and that it would be his first killing. Sam claimed that he never killed a man during all of his unlawful acts. The doctor came back to Sam's shack and told him that he was going to die and that it wouldn't take long at this point.

After Sam's death, his body was taken to the appropriate building as the news was spread that Sam Bass was dead. Sam's body was buried at the Round Rock Cemetery. Sam didn't have more than a couple of people attend his funeral. Frank was later seen in an Arizona Prison where his story wasn't told after that. Jim Murphy lived in fear that the gang members would come back and kill him for his betrayal. A couple of years later, he poisoned himself and died. A few years later, Sam's sister came into Round Rock and placed a nice tombstone over his grave.

This story is a strange one. A man like Sam Bass with all his robberies never killed anyone? It was only speculation that it was his bullet that killed one of the lawmen. It was never proven. Still today you can hear stories about the Black Hills Bandits and the Sam Bass Gang. These are the stories that keep living on. These are the stories of how the west formed.

THIRTEEN

Jim Miller Outlaw or Professional Killer

James Brown was known to be a killer. He was an outlaw, lawman, and professional hitman of his time. Some people saw him as a family man. Some saw him as a ruthless dark soul. Did he kill people because of the job or did he do it because he liked killing? When he was at the end of a noose, he claimed he killed fifty-one men during his life. I'll go more into his story and I'll let you decide what kind of man James was.

James had many names, but the most commonly used were Jim Miller, Killin Jim, and Deacon Jim. He was born on October 25th, 1861, in Van Buren, Arkansas.

His father was Jobab Miller who was born in Pennsylvania in 1801. His father was a stonemason and built some important buildings during his time. His mother was Cynthia "Synthia" Miller from the Basham family. She was born in Arkansas in 1821. His father died and the year is unknown in history but I did find that his body was buried at Alma Cemetery, Crawford Arkansas. After the death, Jim's mother moved the family to Evant, Texas, to live with her parents and family. Jim wasn't new to death because his grandfather and grandmother were found dead, murdered in their own home. The same home where Jim and his mother moved to.

Jim was only eight years old when this took place. Believe it or not, Jim was arrested at that time, even though he was very young. I couldn't find they suspected it was Jim but the court system let him off and didn't press any charges against him. Something most has made the local law enforcement think foul play and Jim was involved. Jim's older sister George and her husband accepted Jim into their home after Jim was released. According to records of the area, Jim and his mother lived here and did for a few years.

In 1884, Jim seemed to be on the killing streak again when his brother-in-law was shot on the porch and died of his wounds. This was his sister's husband that took Jim into their home. Word around town, before the murder, Jim was telling townspeople that he was going to kill John Coop. Jim set up the perfect alibi by going to church and slipping away, unnoticed, he went to the house and shot John with a shotgun. Jim wasn't so lucky this time. He was arrested and brought to the local jail. He was held there during his murder trial. In court, he was convicted of murder and sentenced to life. Jim was seventeen years old.

Later Jim was released due to a technicality and mishap of the court system. Jim was no longer welcome at his family's home and he left. This might have been the best thing for his family because one by one, it seemed Jim was killing them. Killin Jim was not a normal man by this time. He was an evil boy according to many people that knew him. People say that he was smart, too smart for his own good. Many also heard Jim mention and talked about killing at a young age. Some were wounded if he was a son of the devil. He learned that it could avoid jail.

Jim had to start a new life and he was a man in his twenties at this time. At this point Killer Jim was an appropriate name for Jim but he was just getting started. Jim was hired to work as a hired man on the McCulloch County ranch. This is where he started to converse with other outlaws that also work on the ranch and in the area. He spent a lot of his time working and committing petty crimes. Stealing cattle, horses, and small-time thieving. Jim met some of the more known and worse criminals called the Clements Clan. This group was known for killing people and it seemed that Jim was getting deeper and deeper into the path of a very bad man.

After some time, Jim married one of the Clements family members and the daughter of Mannen Clements. Her name was Sallie Clements and also known as Sarah. She was born October 12th, 1871 in McCulloch County Texas. Her father was known to be a bad man that was good with a gun. A gunfighter is how he was seen in Texas and many people would not dare to cross paths with him. He was an outlaw that was arrested by Wild Bill Hickok at one point in his life. He was later released due to a mutual friend of Wild Bill's. Now Jim's new wife wasn't the best citizen herself. It's safe to say that she learned a lot from her dad and carried on much like him.Jim was only becoming more and more of a deadly pistol in this area and he mentioned many times that he couldn't be stopped. Jim and his wife moved to Pecos where he worked at a saloon for some time and after getting to know some local people, they made him a deputy sheriff. They attended the local church and on the outside, they seemed to be a nice little family looking for a good start. Jim's new job seemed to be a respectable one but he wasn't in it for the benefit of making the area a safer place. He wanted the job so he could hide behind his badge and continue the life he knew, killing and working as an outlaw.

It wasn't long until the townspeople noticed that things were changing in their town. Jim wasn't making many arrests and cattle started to come up missing. Some people figured that cattle rustlers were in the area and no one thought about Jim being involved. Why would they? He was the law and protector of the town. Another thing that was strange is that Jim would come back with dead people on the back of his horse. This happened more than arrests were made. The sheriff confronted Jim about all the dead bandits he brought back to town and Jim always had the same story, he was trying to make an arrest and the bandits were trying to shoot him.

He claimed self-defense every single time. After a while, the sheriff stripped him of his badge. This was yet again trouble for the locals. You have to understand. Jim wasn't just committing murders and breaking the law, he was creating one of the first real-time organized criminal groups in the United States. He used his badge to befriend some deep pocket outlaws and they found his sneaky thieving during the time he was a deputy. Jim would have made a great partner with Al Capone. Jim was running organized crimes just like he did. Only this was the wild west, not alcohol. Jim was so far into crime; I don't think he would ever get out of it.

History shows he liked it and it was a great way to use his unwanted and unworthy talent. The crime was at an all-time high in Pecos and that's when the sheriff knew he made the wrong choice in hiring Jim and the right choice by firing him. By this time, too many heavy-hitting outlaws have entered the area. They were not about to forfeit their investments because Jim lost his badge. Jim was becoming the Godfather if you will. Not one man or woman was safe in this town. Neither were the cattle. The outlaws rustled every single cattle herd that came into the area. Money was flowing and Jim was praised. Killer Jim was able to stay out of prison for the reason that many people were scared of him.

The townspeople wouldn't dream of turning into the law. If he was able to scare them, he would pay someone to kill the witness, and sometimes, he just paid them off for the silence. He had this area locked down as no one has ever seen it before in Texas. Don't get it wrong, Jim was still killing but he couldn't keep up with how many people needed to be silenced in the area. The one thing that was getting in Jim's way was the sheriff who took his badge away. Jim wasn't able to continue on with organized crime until he got his badge back.

That's when he came up with the idea that once Bud, the sheriff, came back into town from his traveling, he was going to kill him. Jim arranged for an outlaw to kill Bud. The plan was set up and put into motion. One man was in the background and notified Bud and the officials. When Bud's train landed in town, he was ready and he arrested the men that were supposed to kill him. The only witness that warned Bud was killed later in New Mexico and the law wasn't able to prove that Jim was involved.

The criminals of the area were getting desperate and had a new plan. Bud wasn't going to sit around and let the outlaws take over his town, not after knowing that they were after him. One day, he saw Jim in town, on the street, and without warning, he shot him several times. Bud thought he killed Jim but he was wearing a metal coat that was designed to reflect bullets. Jim did heal from his wounds and he sent the law out for Bud. Here was Bud in court, fighting to explain how Jim is the outlaw and he was trying to save the town.

Because of lack of evidence, Bud was stripped of his badge and he then left town. A few months later, Bud returned to town to visit his family. Jim heard of this and waited until night, entered the saloon, and killed Bud with a shotgun. Some say that Bud's head was nearly gone because the shotgun was so close to his head.

Jim was faced with a jury and they let him go again. Jim was truly untouchable and won the battle once again. Later down the road, something else happened that you may not be able to comprehend. Then again, this is Jim we are talking about and he literally has gotten away with murder, many times. Jim was able to land a job with the Texas Rangers. He moved his family to Fort Worth as soon as he was able to. Sallie, Jim's wife, opened a boarding house in their new town. During this time, Jim advertised that he was a professional killer and he would charge one-hundred and fifty dollars to kill.

Jim was on a rampage and this moment. If someone wanted to have someone dead, just reach out to Jim. He did the same thing that he did with a badge. If he was hired to kill someone, he finished the job and blamed the killings on self-defense. This time, in the new townspeople were not as forgiving. They didn't think of him like the last time and it seems that his luck may change. Contracts were signed and Jim hired a lawyer to keep him out of jail. At one time, Jim had over twelve contracts to kill. He dropped his price and started charging fifty dollars.

Some of the contracts paid more. The more important the person was, the more Jim would charge. One contract awarded him five hundred dollars. Many witnesses ended up missing in the area and many figured that Jim was to blame. Everyone was too afraid to testify. This carried on for far too long and Fort Worth was much like the old town Jim lived in, it was starting to play in his hands. Even Pat Garrett was killed. If this name sounds familiar, that's because he's the lawman that killed Billy the Kid. If you go back to chapter seven, you can refresh your memory. No one could prove that Jim killed Pat but historians are still debating on that.

Pat was thought of as a threat and the outlaws wanted him out of the way. Whether it was Jim or another outlaw, Pat Garrett was dead. Strange how these outlaws and lawmen crossed paths, one way or another from state to state. Now Gus Bobbitt was the next person on the list to be killed. Local outlaws wanted him gone because he was one of the most respected lawmen in the area. He was a threat and a big one to Jim and the other outlaw. Jim expected the contract but on this job, he made a big mistake. As you can see, the lawmen had kept the crime to a minimum, and the outlaws and organized crime leaders wanted to be free of posing threats and Jim was the man to get rid of them.

Jim shot Bobbitt on February 27th, 1909, right in front of his homestead. Bottitt's wife witnessed the murder and Jim left her alive. It's almost like he thought he was invisible and overconfident. Killer Jim made a big mistake. Within a few days, the posse arrested Jim and put him in jail. Some say that he wasn't acting like he was worried about the murder he committed. He sat in jail, asking for nice meals, and carried on like he was going to be released soon. The law even arrested the men that signed the killing contract with Jim. Now four people were sitting in jail for murder. After some time, Jim started to worry because he was in jail longer than he ever had been before.

The courts and the state of Texas were preparing for the trial and the prosecuting attorney was getting ready. Little did anyone know, the town of Fort Worth was ready to take the law into its own hands. A group of townspeople broke into the jail and demanded the keys to Jim's cell. They took him out of the stable and hung the criminals, one at a time. Jim was saved for last. Jim Miller, Killer Jim, was the last of the four, and hangers put the noose around his neck. Jim knew what was coming and that's when he mentioned that he didn't want everyone to forget that he killed fifty-two people in his life.

The townspeople let him talk for a minute and then Jim himself kicked the stool from underneath him, hanging himself. That was it. He was dead moments later. The only person that killed Jim was Jim. He made my list to write about because, in all my research, he may have been the most different. He wasn't like the other outlaws and murderers I've mentioned in this book. Something about him makes me scared, puzzled, and confused, all at the same time.

Jim was the man I believe paved the way for organized crime. It was the turn of the century and Jim was making an example of criminal activity. Was he smart or was he dumb?

Did he really just like killing or did he see the money in it? I'll let you decide as the reader. This is a piece of history that we should all remember. History like this helps us understand the behaviors of criminals and maybe we can be one step ahead of them.

FOURTEEN

Jesse James Rebel or Hero

The story of Jesse James is well known but I want to tell it as I see his story from my research. I've been looking into Jesse's story for some time now. I know that many people think that some of his buried loot is in the area where he lived. This is where I got involved. After learning more about his history, I have to wonder, was it the Civil War that drove him to his outlaw ways? Some people claim that he was nothing but a thief. Some people say he was more of a Robin Hood. Robbing the rich and giving it to the poor. I am a historical researcher and historical treasure hunter and I like to get to the bottom of legends.

This means I use old lost history to find evidence of treasures lost in time. I've spent most of my adult life, chasing after the lost treasures. I've learned that if you really want to find something that is lost, you really need to do your homework and dig much deeper into the legends and old history than most people do. During my research, I discovered that many people think Jesse James, his brother, and even his father were a part of something much larger than robbing banks and trains.

There's talk about Jesse's father being a part of the Freemasons as well as Frank and Jesse. This is where I really dug deep into Jesse and his family's history. Within a short time of researching what I could, I started to find keywords that get me interested and intrigued. Some of those keywords were, KGC, Freemasons, and even the Knights Templar. In all my studies, there's a good chance that these types of subjects make for a very interesting story. Possibly even a huge discovery. Needless to say, I was on the job and I knew I had to learn everything about Jesse to truly see if he was involved with hiding treasures and possibly connected with the KGC and Freemasons.

I'm now convinced that Jesse had placed treasures in and around the states he worked in. Before we get into details about these possible treasures and unspoken history, let's get to his history and go from there. This is his story. Jesse Woodson James was born on September 5th, 1847. He came from a small area near where modern-day Kearney is today. Some people know the area by the name of Little Dixie. Jesse's father was Robert Salle James and he was a Baptist minister and a founder of William Jewell College. He graduated from Georgetown College in 1843 with honors and a Bachelor's Degree in Arts. He then moved on to his Master's degree in Arts.

He was a well-educated man and had a promising future. He was an English and Scottish American and his parents were immigrants. Robert was a man of ambitious ideas and he decided that he wanted to strike it rich in California. He packs his things up and makes his way. Unfortunately, he wasn't there long before he died at Hangtown Gold Camp in California. His grave was left unmarked in a cemetery now known as Placerville California. Robert was given time to prepare for his death which in return was bad for the James family. His death left nothing but heartache and debt.

Jesse was only three years old when he lost his father. The year was 1850. Zerelda James was Jesse's mother and she was born on January 29, 1825, in Woodford County Kentucky. She married Robert James when she was sixteen years old on December 28th, 1841. She gave birth to four children Alexander Franklin James, Robert R. James, Jesse Woodson James, and Susan Lavenia James. After Robert died, she remarried and he was reported to be cruel to Jesse and his brother.

She lost her second husband shortly after due to an accident where he was thrown off his horse. She did get married for the third time and lived her life out until she died of heart failure. She was eighty-six years old. Jesse had an older brother that was born in 1843 and his name was Alexander Franklin James but he was known as Frank in history. Frank was known as a smart kid and he read a lot. Books like William Shakespeare and more. His personality was a bit quieter than his younger brother Jesse's. Frank was known to be a thinker and more than less of the talker in the room.

Jesse would have had a second older brother but Robert R. James died just one month after birth in 1845, two years before Jesse was born. In 1849, Susan Lavenia James was born and she was the baby of the family for some time. That was until Jesse's mother was married for the third time when she gave birth to 4 half siblings Sarah Louisa Samuel, John Thomas Samuel, Fanny Quantrill Samuel, and Archie Peyton Samuel. Jesse is the second youngest child and he was young enough that he didn't get to know his half-siblings as well as he could have. The James family was a normal southern family from Missouri and life was pretty good and so was the farming in this area.

Even though Jesse lost his biological father, and his mother's second husband wasn't very kind to him and Frank, his mother married a more quiet and subtle man and his life went back to normal. This area of Missouri was known to be free and that's what way they wanted it even when the Union started to come west. Their banks, train companies, and money started to change the way the area lived but many of them did not want the new lifestyle. As the towns became larger, the local people started to resist the new ideas of the Yankees. Southerners wanted things and their culture to stay the same while the Union wanted things to change.

This created animosity in the area. Mostly between the original southern people of the area against the new transplants that started to settle in. The new railroad brought in many new jobs, workers, and businesses and it's hard to stop progress when progress wants to be made. The southerners believed that the Yankees were taking away their freedom and livelihood. These were the early signs of civil war coming if they wanted it or not. A couple more years went by and the Union started to become a stranglehold in these parts.

Clay County was a proud and local area to the Confederate ways of thinking and this became the first battleground and they stood their ground to defend their way of life. By 1863 Frank was now a young man, coming out of his teens and he wanted to fight the war against the Yankees. Jesse was fifteen years old and even though he wanted to join his older brother, he was forced to stay and help his mother around the house. The tide of the war was turning against the confederate loyalists of the area. Many of the Yankees would raid homes and intimidate families and farmers of the area. It was known to the Union that the James boy Frank, sided with the Confederates and joined the war. Any family that was leaning towards the Confederacy would find themselves hunted down and harassed by Yankee soldiers.

One day Jesse was outside working their lands when a group of Yankees approached their home. They asked Jesse where his brother Frank was because they wanted to talk with him. Jesse was just a boy at the time and before he knew it, his mother saw what was happening outside and she hurried to tell the soldiers to leave. The soldiers grabbed her husband, Dr. Reuben Samuel, and took him outside by a tree. They tied a noose around his neck and threw the rope around a tree branch. The soldiers were asking where Frank was and when the doctor could tell them, they pulled on the rope and hanged him by his neck.

They then led off after a few moments and then continued to do the same thing to him. Over and over again, they tortured him, and Jesse and his mom were right there, watching the whole thing. The soldiers finally stopped pulling on the rope and decided to leave the home when they didn't get their whereabouts. This made Jesse a young man and one thing these soldiers didn't see coming was the James family. Jesse and his family had no idea where Frank was. All they knew is that he was fighting in the war. Jesse knew that the soldiers were just being ruthless and heartless so he did what Jesse does for the rest of his life. He would never allow someone to do something like this to him or his family again.

From this point, he took care of any problems and threats in his way. This was a moment of reckoning. Jesse wasn't going to sit back and allow his family to be treated like this. Not in their own home and land at the hands of the Yankees. Jesse decided that he wanted to go to war and teach the Union a lesson but not before he took care of some business in town. The next day, Jesse took his gun and went to the house of one of the Yankee soldiers that mistreated his family. He wanted to settle the score once and for all. He walked up to the door, knocked, and when the Yankee answered it, he told the man to pray. Pray like it really matters because he was about to die.

Jesse then shot and killed the Yankee, right where he stood at the doorway. Jesse was fifteen years old when he killed his first man. After arranging with the Confederate recruiters, Jesse was assigned to fight alongside his older brother Frank. The Civil War was terrorizing the county and the Confederates were doing everything they could to fight back. The Civil War wasn't one large battle in one place, no, the Civil War went on for years from 1861 - 1865. Battles can and go. Some of them prior to 1861 and some of them later than 1865. Frank and Jesse were a part of the conventional armies that fought differently than you may recognize.

You may watch movies of the Civil War that show and explain two different armies, the Union and the Confederates, shooting their guns in an open field at each other. One side would wear blue coats while the other side would wear gray coats. This was the more traditional way of war, but Frank and Jesse were a part of a different type of strategy called guerrilla warfare. It was more of smaller groups that conducted raids against the opposing side. Usually conducted by civilians using military tactics by ambushing when the other side was not expecting it. Jesse, his brother, and the rest of their group would ride their horse on the outside of the main trails and scout for Yankees, sitting at camp, riding down the road, and even eating dinner. They would wait for the right time, ride in with their horses, and shoot as many Yankees as they could.

The other element that helped Jesse, Frank, and the other guerrillas were their guns. Back in those days, it was common for the soldiers to have a piston and rifles but most of them were single-shot firearms. Jesse and his team had multiple-shot revolvers and this made it easier to win these small battles. Most of them had a couple of revolvers, loaded and ready to go when they attacked. With a few men, they were able to shoot many more bullets than the Yankees. This gave them an advantage on the field.

This was a quick in-and-out assignment. They would ride in with their guns drawn and ready to fire, point and shoot, and get the hell out. This worked very well for Jesse and his group. Many of them were able to make an impact and escape without harm. The surprise of war is where they thrived. This continued to be the way Jesse fought throughout his time. It also helped Jesse become a man that can think on his feet very quickly. He was learning how to be fast and accurate with his guns.

I think it's safe to say that Jesse may have learned to be somewhat of a savage during this time as well. It's said that guerrilla warfare would consist of killing civilian unionists, and prisoners of war, and some say they would even scalp some of the murdered victims. It's reported that Jesse and Frank killed a lot of people during these times. If you ask me, the war turned Frank and Jesse into full-blown killers. One of their leaders/captains was named Bloody Bill Andresen and his name says it all. He liked to hurt people. Some say that he would cut off the heads and other body parts of his victims.

Jesse and Frank were involved with one of the worst types of men and I'm thinking that they became numb to this type of behavior. They were a force to be reckoned with for sure. I would like to tell you how long Jesse fought in the war but history shows he never stopped fighting. It's said that he fought for roughly three years. Even when the Union claimed victory, Jesse and Frank continued on like it never stopped. What happened next may cause a disagreement between the way people think about outlaws and people that had a hard life. Can their bad choices be justified?

Times were different, as you have heard me say in this book but Jesse was tired of his family being targeted by the Union. I think the James family was a little bit of both. Frank James fell ill during the war and he was sent back to his family's home. Jesse stayed back with his team to continue fighting. When word got out that Frank was back in town, the opposing side came up with a plan to kill a James boy once and for all. A few men approached James's family home in the dark of the night.

They had a bomb and they planned on using it. Jesse's mom, stepfather, and little brother were in the house that night. The men crept up to the window, lit the fuse, and threw it inside the house. When the bomb went off, metal shrapnel from the bomb and material from the home blasted the living room section of the house. Jesse's mom and brother were in that room. After the blast, Jesse's father-in-law ran into the room and saw that his young son and wife were on the floor. The room was destroyed and blood from his family was spilling everywhere. He kneeled down and noticed that his son was dead and that his wife's arm was blown off.

Panicked and angry, he grabbed his long rifle and ran out the door, shooting in every direction. The bombers were running away in the night, through the brush and trees. He continued firing until his gun was empty. Frank wasn't home that night. He was the main target for the Union and now, with their brother dead and mother losing her arm, the Union just declared war on the James boys. Jesse's family did leave Clay County after this due to the events that happened on the property. At the age of seventeen, Jesse suffered two gun wounds that affected his war abilities but he still kept going out of anger.

Frank was separated from Jesse and he continued on with the war until it was over. No matter how well Jesse and his team of Confederates fought, the Union was still declared the winner. This still divided the states into three different parties. A document that I found from 1860, from the University of California at Santa Barbara, explained from a political perspective what happened to the Union and the Confederate States of America after the war. It claims that many of the Unionists moved to the Democratic party and Confederates moved alongside the Republican party. The third party was indecisive and moved towards the Independent party.

Now that doesn't mean that if you were a Yankee you became a Democrat or vice versa overnight or indefinitely, it just means the majority did so. This was still hard in the north and south. The war was over but the fight kept going on. The thing was if you wanted to keep your lands, and a respectable job like a pastor, or public office, you couldn't vote either. The control in the new world was over-whelming to many and many lost their livelihoods. You had to prove that you sided with the Union before the war. Sometimes it was neighbors disagreeing or maybe family members but there was still a great divide in our country.

It just wasn't called the Civil War anymore. Because of this, anyone who stood up to the opposing site has been declared a hero for speaking their mind. If someone disagreed with you, then you were an outcast. This virus cycle continued for quite some time and it gave Jesse the underhand in his state and surrounding states. Because of this divide, Jesse and his newly started gang were able to play the rule of regulars in some eyes while they were becoming outlaws in others.

Jesse caught up to his brother Frank after the war and they lived out in the wilderness and to them, the war wasn't gone. They carried on just like they did before but now, things have changed in their eyes. They want to hit the Union where it hurts and taking money from their businesses and banks were sounding pretty good to these confederate men. They came up with a plan to rob a Union train. The owners and the contents of value were from Yankee loyalists.

Jesse needed some men and they had a good idea of who to use to pull off this train robbery. They hoped that no one would expect it and they were right. Jesse and Frank rounded up their men and the plan worked out perfectly.

They knew right where to stop the train. It was the perfect place. No one was anywhere around to help, especially the law. The train was stopped by the gang and they went right to work. They went straight for the safes and they found enough money to hold them off for months and months. Sixty-thousand dollars was taken from the train but the gang wasn't done yet.

The gang decided to hit the passenger cars too. This wasn't your everyday robbery. Jesse took the lead and as they entered the cars, Jesse asked for a show of hands. "How many of you fought in the war?" Then he asks "How many of you are Confederate friendly?" He wasn't done, then he asks if there were any widows from the war. You see, Jesse may have had a heart and he was very careful from robbing people with the same beliefs as him.

When someone raised their hands, Jesse ordered his men to not rob them. Now, if he saw that a rich man didn't raise his hand, then he was robbed. Jesse one hundred percent wanted to only take from the Yankees. He knew there was enough money from that category and why steal from people like him? The gang took all the loot they wanted and they made a clean getaway. As Jesse and his men were leaving, he handed a letter to a train worker. It was an article Jesse wrote about him, his men, and the train robbery.

If news companies were going to write about the robbery, he wanted to control what was said. Overnight, Jesse and his gang were flaring up the United States. Everyone was able to read about what they did. The money, how they treated the passengers, everything was there. This is where these newly trained robbers earned their name, The James-Younger Gang. The gang started to gain a reputation and to the Union, it was bad but to the southerners, they started to look at his gang as heroes. The James Younger Gang would ride into a southern town and be praised and protected by the town. It really made it easy to continue these robberies.

This outlaw gang didn't just rob trains, they also robbed Union banks as well. They would start to rob banks that were known for having Yankee money in them. For the James Younger Gang, they were becoming celebrities more and more. Some of these robberies would bring in anywhere from ten thousand dollars and more every time. The gang was becoming very wealthy and they liked to show it off. They would go into a loyal town, drink, and spend a lot of money. This helped these small southern towns proper during their time of need.

Something else happens that you may not expect a typical outlaw group to do either. The James Younger Gang was known to also be sympathetic and giving to their most loyal. Stories of the gang giving people money when they needed were spreading around the southern states. This is where they got the Robin Hood figure. So now you have this gang that is robbing money from rich and powerful Union people and companies and then on the other hand you have the southern states admiring them for it, this was historic. The Union did not know how to stop the gang. The typical raiding of homes and trying to intimidate the common people did not work.

The southern people would not turn Jesse or his gang members in, no matter how much of a bounty was placed on their heads. Robberies continued to happen, not just in Missouri but the gang was traveling in surrounding states as well. This also kept the law from tracking them down. It was hard to plan what their next move would be and where. The James Younger Gang were very smart in their tactics. Some think that Frank James was more of the planner and thinker as Jesse was more of the plan executioner. Whenever the gang rode into a town to rob a bank, they would post some of their men on the outside of town to look for trouble during these heists.

Another thing they did that really threw off the law was changing their clothes. They would ride into town wearing an outfit then ride out of town and change their clothes. That way when they are on the road, the law wouldn't recognize them by their descriptions given by witnesses in town. Believe it or not, it worked. There have been stories passed down by the gang that the law would approach them miles and miles away and not stop them. Very smart and if other outlaws would have practiced this more, they may have gotten away more often. I think it's time to mention the gang members' names now.

- Jesse James
- Frank James
- Jim Younger
- John Younger
- Bob Younger

- Cole Younger

Some of the gang members were only used on occasion and some were more temporary. These men's names were:

- John Jarrette
- Clel Miller
- Arthur McCoy
- Matthew Nelson
- Charlie Pitts
- Bill Chadwell

Most of these men knew each other from the war. They trusted and fought together and that made this gang very strong. During this time Chicago was being notified of the robberies and there was one man that the Union thought could put an end to the James Younger Gang. One man was good at tracking down outlaws. Allan Pinkerton. If this name sounds familiar that's because it should. I mention him and his company several times in this book. He was the founder of the Pinkertons and he prided himself on arresting his man. He and his company are private investigators and they have been used for many jobs that seem too hard for the typical lawman.

In fact, Allan Pinkerton only took on some of the hardest criminals known in the world. His men were sometimes used to protect Abraham Lincoln, not the night he was shot, unfortunately. He also took many contracts for the railroad companies to protect the cargo and find the people robbing them. His men were also used to track down and hunt the worst of the worst outlaws. Pinkertons were feared by many bandits and outlaws. Around this time, Allan decided to keep his investigation and business busy only taking on the role of arresting the top ten most wanted in the United States. The James Younger Gang was one of those ten.

He sent a few of his men to Missouri and the surrounding states to find Jesse and his gang. Word started to spread that the Pinkertons were after them and Jesse did the opposite of what other outlaws did before him. He didn't run and hide from them, he sought them out.

One by one, Pinkertons were killed and the gang would leave notes of the dead man to provoke Allan. This happened for a long time. Allan would send more men and better men and they would be found months later, dead.

Some of the Pinkertons tried to outsmart Jesse but that ended in chaos and death too. One Pinkerton tried to pose as an outlaw, to blend in and try to get in with Jesse, and the gang back Jesse was too smart for him too. The gang caught on very quickly and killed him too. It appeared at the time that Jesse and his men were untouchable and in many ways, they were. Not many outlaws and thieves were able to carry on for more than a few years but the James brother was able to rob and carry on for sixteen years.

That's about the longest time that I've researched any outlaw to continue raiding, killing, and robbing. I wonder if Jesse was really good at what he did or if it was straight hatred that pushed him along. Realistically, I think it was both. The James gang were surely able to run wild and rob as much and as often as they wanted. The James Younger Gang still had the heart of many and the hatred of the opposing side. The news was still spreading around the nation and people waited around just to see what the gang was up to next. Newspapers around the country were writing about the robberies. It wasn't until one of their gang members was arrested after a train robbery that changed the way the gang functioned. This was a new gang member and many wondered today how Jesse allowed him to join.

After his arrest, Hobbs Kerry told the law everything they wanted to know. Hobbs snitched about the gang hideouts, what routes they took, and details of Jesse and Frank. He even mentioned that Jesse and Frank had secret hand signals to communicate. These secret hand signs are why some people think that the James brothers and their father were connected with the Freemasons. Were they created by the James family or where they connected to something even bigger? We'll get to all the later in this book.

Now that the law, Pinkertons, and Union people knew all this information, the gang decided that it wasn't safe. For one of the first times in their operations, the gang fled to new grounds to stay undetected. On September 7th, 1876, the James Younger Gang rode into a new town. This town was Northfield in Minnesota. When the gang rode into town, the townspeople were suspicious of the gang. A few things stuck out about them. For one thing, this was a farming and ranching community. Most people rode into this town with a buggy or wagon. The gang all rode in on horses. That townspeople sat back and observed.

The James gang wasted no time to locate a bank that had a lot of Union money in it. This bank was the First National Bank of the area. The gang did what they always did in the past, leaving men outside to watch for dangers as a few men went inside. The outlaws that were inside went straight to the man with the keys to the vault. A lot of fussing and yelling began to happen inside the bank and caused alarm to the townspeople once again. As the gang members were arguing with the bank employee, the townspeople grabbed their guns. The fight broke out and the townspeople started to shoot the gang members outside.

They were yelling, "They're robbing the bank," over and over again. The more gunshots that were fired, the more townspeople came to the bank with their guns. During this time, the robbers inside were growing tired of the bank employee, not giving them his vault key. After some manhandling, one of the outlaws drew a big knife on the banker. One of the gang members came into the bank stating that the townspeople were fighting back and they had to leave. The gang member gets frustrated and shoots the banker, killing him on sight.

When the gang gained control of their emotions, they noticed that a couple of their members were laying in the streets dead. Jesse, Frank, and the rest of the gang got on their horses and shot their way out of town. They barely escape themselves. The gang was never the same after that. Jesse and Frank were later seen a couple of months later in Nashville, Tennessee, and they recruited a few new gang members. Jesse was determined to not be stopped and frankly, I think he liked the lifestyle and didn't know what else to do.

Robberies, life on the run, and death continued to follow the James brothers and their gang. A few stores were robbed by the gang but they didn't payout as much as their brother was used to. In some of these robberies, they only stole around two thousand dollars. This was still a lot of money and it amounts to about forty-five thousand dollars to the present time. The money was still keeping the gang on the run but they were definitely hiding at this point from the law and Pinkertons.

The James boys did not feel safe, even in their own home state so Jesse moved his family, wife, and kids to St. Joseph Missouri and Frank moved to Virginia, where it was safer for him. This was the time that the two brothers said goodbye to each other and they said that they were getting out of the life of crime. They both took on different names and tried to blend in with their new lives. I'm almost coming to the end of this story. This is the part of the story that is well talked about. Movies and books have been written about Jesse's death. I'll go into it a little to finish.

Jesse was thirty-four years old now. His new life changed him. It's like he was there but his mind was not. It's said that he was quiet around his two children and his wife. He spent a lot of time sitting in his rocker chair at home in the evenings. Jesse and his family were still on the run and his true identity. This caused the James family to move often to new homes and towns. He went by the name Thomas Howard and he claimed that he was a businessman, making money as a cattleman. He was looked at by the communities he lived in as a rich man. He spent most of his days in town, meeting and visiting with townspeople.

The men around him noticed that he was something special. Even though he was a killer and robber, he could draw in a crowd and mingle with the best of them. He still was not able to stop the life of an outlaw so he kept around him a few men to carry out whatever crime he felt that he could pull off. The Ford brothers were the only men he trusted at the time with his real identity. Their names were Charley and Robert Ford. This was the last mistake Jesse ever made. Jesse, his family, and the Ford brothers moved again. Jesse and Charley did commit a few small robberies here and there. This was the way that Jesse was able to continue his rich status.

The biggest thing is that the other Ford brother, Robert, also known as Bob, was working with the local Governor to bring Jesse to justice. Robert betrayed Jesse and it was only a matter of time before Jesse would be arrested. To fast forward this timeline, Jesse was becoming suspicious of the Ford Brothers. One of Jesse's gang members was just arrested and he read about it in the newspaper. He knew that only the Ford brothers knew the information that would lead to his member's arrest. Jesse knew that his outlaw days were at their end. He didn't want to live the life of a prisoner or even worse, a rope that would hang him to his death.

Jesse was a man that could not go out that way and he wanted to die the way he chose. April 3rd, 1882 was the day that Jesse made his decision. After having breakfast with the Ford brother, Jesse did something that would still puzzle people today. He sat up from the dinner table and acted very strange. The Ford brothers noticed that Jesse took off his gun belt and announced it to them out loud. Jesse never looked them in the eyes. He remained to look forward in the other direction.

The Ford brothers have never seen Jesse without his guns. Jesse never let his guard down like this and Robert took advantage of the moment. Then Jesse grabbed a feather duster and pointed to a painting in the living room and said, "Don't the picture look dusty?" He then walked up to it with his back to the Ford brothers and Robert took out his gun, pointed it at Jesse, and fired, killing him. Jesse's wife and children were home and they all heard what happened. This was the end of Jesse.

This is where Robert Ford's story comes into play. I will not write any more about him. He was a man that shot a man with his back turned. He was seen in the future as a coward. Jesse claimed in his life that he killed seventeen people in all. That's including his war killings. He died a well-respected man in his community and many people hated his killers, the Ford brothers. He was still a strong southern man with his southern beliefs when he died. He was a true Confederate in his option and he died one too. I guess you can say that he fought for what he thought was right.

I can tell you that many historians and treasure hunters believe that Jesse and his gang were taking so much money, they buried a lot of it all over the place. Union gold, silver, bonds, coins, and paper money. Towards the end of this book, I'll explain the ins and outs of what I've discovered and researched. If you're in the surrounding state of Missouri, and you have the adventurer soul in you, I would certainly keep reading this book. I'll leave breadcrumbs of knowledge and information for you.

FIFTEEN

Felipe Espinosa, Serial Killer

From my experience, if you want the real history of someone or something from Mexico, you need to go straight to the source. North America is good at telling stories within a boundary that it feels comfortable with. I chose Felipe Espinosa because I couldn't find much on him when I first heard his name. This made me want to know more about him and why he was motivated to go on a killing spree. I think you have already learned from this book that not all of these outlaws were born bad and killed just for pleasure. Some of them didn't kill anyone and some of them only robbed people they felt were bad people themselves. Let me explain Felipe's story and then you can understand him better.

Now understand that it's the American men he killed and American lawmen that hunted him down. Why don't we have information on Felipe? Unfortunately, that's the way it worked with old history and many records were hard to find between Mexico and North America after the great war. So this is going to be a much shorter story that mostly begins in Colorado. I'll do my best to tell you the beginning part of his life.

Felipe was born in 1832 and even though some disagree where it's known that he was born in the territory that moved within the

United States boundaries. Some believe his home city was Santa Fe de Nuevo Mexico which is in the northern part of New Mexico in Rio Arriba County. Other people think he was born in Veracruz City, which is much further south in Mexico. Either way, when he was born he was in Mexico and this makes him a Mexican, not an American. In American history, we call him a Mexican-American. His father was Pedro Ignacio Espinosa and there's not much to tell about his history because it's very limited in American history.

I do know that he was born in 1795 in Abiquiu New Mexico territory. He was father to four to seven children and he died in 1858. His mother was Maria Gertrudis Chavez and she gave birth to four to seven children. I can't confirm one hundred percent that all children were biological but I do know from the census how many children lived with them. Some of their names are Maria Tomasa Espinosa and Jose Vivian Espinosa. The rest of the names I couldn't find. This is where his history has a huge gap in it and it didn't start back up again until a few years later when Felipe was a young man.

I'm going to go into some history of the men that are involved with Felipe's story after on in his life. Thomas Tate Tobin was born in 1823 and later on in his young adult life, he was known to be an adventurer, tracker, trapper, and U.S. Scout. We'll call him Tobin. By 1846, Tobin married Pascuala Bernal when they were in the Arroyo Hondo area near Taos. Tobin was involved with the Taos Revolt but not really by choice. He was a man that was in the wrong place at the wrong time but within a few days, he was recruited as a scout to track down and hunt the enemies of war. By 1847, he worked as a higher leader and organized a group.

He was now a scout, guide, and Indian fighter for the U.S. and he spent most of his time advising the U.S. troops and helping them track down Indian tribes. During this time, Tobin was also contracted by the main railroad companies to help them scout out and choose the routes for the train tracks coming from the east and the west. This was just before the Civil War was about to break out from north to south. He had the skills of a mountain man and he was good at fighting off hostile Indians. His work with the railroads went on until the early 1860s. He spent a lot of his time in unknown and unexplored terrains. Tobin was involved with Wild Bill Hickok for a while before Wild Bill moved to Deadwood, South Dakota.

In the season of Spring, Felipe Espinosa was back into the picture of history. He traveled up to and around the territory of Colorado. Felipe was known to be around a lot of knowns and feared murderers of his time. When he came into the area of Colorado, he was already known as "The Bloody Espinosas" and later he was also known as "The Axeman of Colorado." Felipe was married and had two kids at this time. One boy and one girl but he wasn't around his hometown anymore. He was continuing the killing spree that he started in the Mexican-American War.

Felipe was not a murderer or killer after the war until he settled in Colorado and he waited until 1863 to commit his first murder there. Some people of the old days claim that the war caused Felipe to have mental issues. He saw a lot of horrible things and he also was involved with many unforgetting events during the war. His mind was still in the war, even years after it was over. Moving to 1863, Colorado residents and lawmen were faced with a graphic scene of blood and death. Some men were killed on a mountain hillside and many people were surprised to see this type of killing spree.

The law scratched their heads, wondering if it was a band of outlaws that committed the murders or if it was local Indians rebelling. After the murders, many outlooks and scouts were posted in the area but it made it hard for them to find the killers because they had no idea what or who they were looking for. Another victim was discovered not long after in a different location. He was found mutilated and his heart cut out of his chest. This worried the town and the surrounding area. They knew that something was wrong in the area and that a dangerous killing was out to do more.

During the same year, twenty-five more murders were committed, and even though there were some witnesses, no one could describe the killers with enough description to set the law on their trail. It wasn't until a wagon was attacked by these vicious killers that the driver of the wagon was able to escape from the fight. He was able to give a good explanation to the authorities and that's when the State of Colorado finally knew who to look for. The descriptions narrowed down to Felipe, his cousins, and his gang. These soldiers of the old war were on a massive killing spree.

It was at this time that I learned that the Blood Espinosas Gang wasn't just killing people without a reason. It may not be a good reason but just like Jesse James' story, the war changed Felipe and his gang. During the Mexican-American war, Felipe and his group witnessed six of their family members killed. They were not just killed in the matter of war, they were abused and punished for being Mexican during this time. The six family members were brutally killed and some say that the soldiers had their way with the women before they were killed. Felipe and his family members wanted revenge against the U.S.

It wasn't just their family that was killed but their whole town was killed by the U.S. Navy. The Navy ships fired at the townsite and the shells killed and destroyed their town. The townspeople that were not killed by the cannon, were later killed by hand-to-hand combat. Even though Felipe and his men were good fighting soldiers at that time, they were too few men to stop the U.S. Navy. Felipe wanted to get back to the country responsible for the death of women and children during the war. This town was slaughtered and Felipe was going to forget this. Either way his men.

There's more to the story as well. After the war, the Mexican people agreed to a land grant, signed and agreed upon by the U.S. and Mexico. Felipe and his gang felt like the bargain wasn't being held up by the U.S. Felipe and his gang were not shy and they told everyone that the U.S. was not standing by their agreements. The gang felt that they were in their right and they were standing up for what was right and what was wrong. Back to Felipe's mental state. Felipe wasn't afraid to tell his men about a vision that came to him from the Virgin Mary.

He said that she came to him and told him to kill one hundred people for every family member he lost in the war. According to Felipe, he needed to kill at least six hundred people before his mission was over. His gang wasn't afraid to tell people about Felipe's vision and word spread around the territory. It is worse. Felipe was given the news that his wife and daughters were raped and killed by American soldiers. This only fueled the rage within Felipe and his gang. Events started to continue when Felipe's brother killed an American soldier that killed his wife four days prior.

Then a couple of days later, American soldiers came back to the family's ranch to kill the rest of Felipe's family members. I think you can agree that these events would place anyone in a state of mind that would not be beneficial to sociality. Felipe wasn't a soldier of war any longer, he was out to get revenge on his family. Times were different as I mentioned in this book. Some men would sit back and accept what happened and try to move on with their lives. Some men picked up their guns and hunted down the people involved. That was the path Felipe took and it would only end the way that most do, murder, running from the law, and death.

Felipe and his gang wrote a letter to Governor John Evans. In this letter, Felipe explains and threatens to kill six hundred men and the Governor himself unless he would grant five thousand acres in Colorado to him. Instead of the Governor trying to make peace and come up with an agreement with Felipe, he sent the U.S. Cavalry out to track him and his gang down. Felipe took this as an act of war and the murders continued and so did small battles. Somewhere along these battles, Felipe's brother was killed. At this point, he lost almost everyone close to him and nothing was going to stop him now.

This is where Tom Tobin came into the scene. He was hired to track and hunt down Felipe and his gang of killers. Tobin used his skills of tracking to find the hiding location of the outlaw gang. Tobin was given fifteen soldiers to help him not only find the Bloody Espinosas but to kill them on location. Now, this is where the story takes a turn in a different direction once again. Tobin just happened to be a cousin of the Espinosas. Even though he was contracted to find Felipe, he didn't tell anyone about the family ties. One day, Tobin left his camp early in the morning and he didn't take his soldiers with him. Only a young Mexican boy went with him.

Tobin was gone for a few days and he did return with a sack of heads. Claiming that they were the heads of Felipe and Julian. When asked why he left his soldiers and why he went after the gang by himself, he stayed off-ish and didn't really explain his actions. It's said that he was friendly with Felipe and his men during the time he found them. Tobin came into their camp, talked, and drank with them until everyone was asleep. That's when Tobin killed and cut their heads off. Tobin asked for the bounty fees for the death of Felipe at a later time. He was given only one thousand five hundred dollars instead of the known reward amount of two thousand and five hundred dollars.

In today's world, it is believed that this was a simple situation that led to a very bad killing spree. It could have been avoided if both parties had abided by the rules of war. No soldier should attack the opposing side's family at their home. This caused Felipe to grow his rage. When it comes to the agreement of the land, this is not the first time I found evidence of an agreement between two parties and one side doesn't hold up their end of the deal. Some people say this was due to the taxes and the money it brings into the U.S.

I'm not sure what the full cause was for this war but I'm pretty sure it has to do with the change of culture, land, and behavior of the old west. The Mexican people were forced to change their way of thinking after the U.S. took their lands. This could very much be like the story of the U.S. taking the lands away from local Indian tribes as well. Even though history is written to show that everyone else was the rebels and savages of the land, it makes me wonder. Was the U.S. responsible for the acts of the natives?

Mexican and Indian? The bottom line is that this was their land before it was ours. The U.S. government took what it wanted and expected the natives to change and adapt their cultures and way of life. I think this story shows that this way of thinking only works if you do what some people call cancel culture. Did we bring on much of the tragic situations to ourselves by being terrorists? Think about that. The natives were here before we were. If someone came into our lands now and tried to take it, what would we do?

I would love to go into this story more with you but plain and simple, much of the history wasn't explained or written. Perhaps that was done on purpose.

SIXTEEN

Henry Plummer Prospector, Lawman, and Outlaw

This is another story of a lawman that used his badge to conduct outlaw outbreaks. While he acted as the sheriff of Bannack Montana, he was accused of being the leader of an outlaw gang known as the Innocents. This gang was big on robbing and looting shipments coming from Virginia City and the owners and stockholders weren't going to sit back and allow this type of behavior to happen any longer. Some say that there's still treasure hidden in the area he lived and worked. I think we can discover more information by learning about Henry's life. This is his story.

Henry Handy Plummer was born in 1832 in Addison Maine and he was one of six siblings in his family. His father was William Jeremiah and he died when Henry was still in his teenage years. I couldn't find much in my records about his father. He must have been a simple man in those days. I did find out that his father was a sea captain and he hoped Henry would follow his family career. Henry had a condition that made it hard for him to be at sea. He would become cold and start shivering in the ocean and he learned very quickly that the sea life would not work for him. His mother was Elizabeth Plummer and she had a hard time financially when her husband died.

Henry tried to stay and help his mother for as long as he dared but his spirit was telling him to head west. The Gold Rush of California was becoming something that dreams were made of and Henry educated himself and prepared himself as much as he could, prior to leaving his family's home in Maine. Before he left home, he told his mother that he would go west, start mining, and strike it rich so he could fix their money issues. He promised his mother that he would be back after he accomplished that. The trip from Maine wasn't the easiest.

He had to travel by boat, which made it hard for him. They arrive at the Panama Channel by horse, then get on another ship that would take them to California. This trip took him almost a month and finally, he arrived in San Francisco. This wasn't where he wanted to be. It was more of a stepping stone to get him out to the hills, looking for gold. He did land a local job where he was able to save his money. After some hard work, and a little luck, he was able to save enough money to travel once again.

This time, he decided to head in the north direction to the State of Nevada. This area was a promising place where many miners before him found gold and a lot of it. Henry did never do well for himself in Nevada. It appears that he learned that money can be made in and around the mining process and not only in the gold itself. He did mine for a while and he invested his money into a mining claim. After a year or so, he was able to get away from mining by trading his stock in the claim and purchased a ranch and bakery where he then shifted his hard work in that direction.

When he was in San Francisco, he worked at a bakery and I think he found that he was better doing that line of work than mining. He must have been a smart man because many people traveled west and came back empty-handed. Not Henry. He was doing pretty well for himself at a very young age. Now he was a businessman. Keep in mind that he didn't give up all his shares on the mine. He kept some and that made him an owner of three businesses. History goes to show that he was a likable man in the town of Nevada City. He was trusted and looked up to by many. Success can be a powerful thing to admire and trust comes along with it.

In total, he was only in Nevada City for two years before the town started to talk about electing him as the local sheriff and city manager. During this time, the talk was going around about Henry and how he should think about running in office and politics as a Democrat. That never happened but it goes to show you that Henry was doing good for himself. As you can see, Henry was a busy man with plenty on his plate. His future was looking bright and in his favor. The problem for him was that he was too aggressive for his own good. As you can see, he liked money and success, and being the law in the area met he was in control.

He could control the narrative, he could control the new laws, and he could hide any wrongdoing that may accrue. He did all the above. By the time he was twenty-four years old, he became the Marshal of what was the third largest city in the state. This made plenty of opportunities for Henry. He ended up getting into the wrong crowd of people. These people were not called outlaws but they may have been worse. They didn't go into the bank or saloon, giving away their identity robbing the place. No, this was organized crime at its finest. Let the small-time criminals run free and attract attention to themselves, while we make money underground is where he was heading.

This way of life didn't last long. He was a little bold with his life and he was sleeping around with a miner's wife. The husband confronted Henry and a duel was selected to settle the argument. The end results landed Henry as the victor and the miner was laying on the ground dead. This landed trouble for Henry and he was arrested for murder. During court, they dismissed the charges, only to reopen them and he was then found guilty and sentenced to ten years in prison. Henry always claimed it was self-defense but the courts didn't see it that way. He started his sentence on February 22nd, 1859 but he didn't stay in prison long.

The local people of Nevada City petitioned the Governor and asked that he would be set free and their wishes came true. Henry was released in a short amount of time. By August 16th, 1859 Henry was released. He returned to Nevada City but he soon learned that his life would not be the same. His small group of bandits was still running around, committing their crimes. Henry and his bandits were getting bolder and they robbed a stagecoach and Henry was identified. Henry was back in the court system and this time, the courts couldn't keep him in jail for long. Because of the lack of evidence in the court, Henry was set free.

Henry could stay out of trouble and it was coming looking for him now. He shot and killed another man and this time, he wasn't going to take the risk. He escaped from jail Now, Henry was on the run, heading toward Oregon. He was a wanted man and just like many wanted men, they continue their life of crimes to stay out of jail. Henry became friends with another bandit named Jim Mayfield. Jim was a wanted man as well and the both of them decided to stay on the run. They ended up in Lewiston Idaho. Henry and Jim were trying to lay low and blend in with the town. The year was 1862 and he worked at the local casino until he saw a familiar face, Cy Kinner, his old cellmate. This part of Idaho wasn't safe now because Henry and Cy decided to start a gang, robbing people and targeting mainly gold miners.

He couldn't stay out of trouble and ended up killing another man while wandering between Elk City and Lewiston Idaho. This man was a saloon keeper. The saloon keeper's name was Patrick Ford. Patrick mostly had a death wish because after he kicked them out, he followed them outside and started to shoot at them. Henry pulled his gun out and returned fire, killing Patrick. This was a lot of trouble for Henry because Patrick's friends created a mod to go after Henry. Trouble was brewing very fast the outlaws skipped town and left for good.

In the beginning stages of winter in 1862, Henry wanted to head back home. He was feeling sicker and sicker and he felt that it was time. He had tuberculosis and there was not much to escape it. Winter came in hard and he wasn't able to travel over the mountains as he hoped. He was forced to work at the Sun River Ranch to make ends meet. During this time, Henry met a woman, and they wasted no time getting married. He was a man of spontaneous manners at this point. Later Henry moved to Bannack Montana to start mining once again. This area was booming with success.

While he started settling in, he noticed that with the Civil War happening, the town was manless and lawless, and it seemed to be easy pickings. Many men in town were more focused on mining, not outlaws and bandits. Henry decided to start another gang and this time, this gang would be remembered as the Innocents. They started to rob all the miners and their gold that came in and out of the area. This gang became large very quickly and feared too. He couldn't stay out of trouble and he killed another man in the area again. This time, the law wasn't anywhere around and he was able to stay in town.

By this time, over ten thousand miners were hunting and tracking down gold in the area. The place was booming and Henry was around the town long enough to become a familiar face. He remembered that being a lawman worked well for him in Nevada City and he turned on his charms once again when the town was looking for a sheriff. Believe it or not, he was appointed. There was some bad dealing involved and his opponent did leave town suddenly but nevertheless, he was sheriff once again. This gave the Innocents the upper hand and the gang grew to almost a hundred strong.

This is much larger than most gangs of their time. It was possible because the sheriff wasn't stopping the gang, he was the leader and mastermind. The crime was on the rise and the townspeople couldn't believe it. How can outlaws be so strong in the area and even increase after they appointed a sheriff? After about four months, Bannack was in a bad place and something had to be done. Train and stagecoach robberies were occurring, along with banks too. The wealthy business owners of the railroad and banks from the East hired a man to help find the outlaws and bring them to justice. A man named Matt Clark, a railroad detective, was hired by a private company to get to the bottom of these crimes. He was looking to track down why these robberies have happened in the last three months.

As Matt was making his way through the territory, one of the Innocent Gang members caught word and rode into Bannak to let Henry know he was coming. So the gang did what they were good at, stopped the stagecoach that Matt was on and they tried to kill him and his men. There was another man named Franky that was placed at the train office to get information about the day-to-day of the railroad's operation. When Matt got into town, he was greeted by Henry and they both played off what happened. Matt wanted to leave because he was in town secret and he told everyone that he was there to mine.

Henry acted like he had no idea why Matt and his men were attacked. He blamed it on the local outlaws. This was quite the operation by the Innocent gang. They had all the inside information they needed and the sheriff on their side. Matt was smart and he didn't want anyone to know that he was going to sit back and watch everyone with a suspecting eye. After some time, Matt was starting to suspect Henry of the crimes but he tried to hide his intuition. Matt was in the area when a man was murdered and Henry came out with his deputy to act as if he didn't know what happened.

Matt told Henry that the killer couldn't be more than fifteen minutes' ride away and the law rode off to find them. One thing that Matt noticed is many of the deputies and Henry would wear a handkerchief, all in the same fashion around their necks. This seemed strange to Matt. Things were cracking down on the Innocent gang and Henry. Matt continued on with his investigation and started to see that the town was overrun by suspicious people and that the sheriff wasn't very fast in getting the criminals. He even mentioned to a townsperson that he can see why the area is overrun with crime. The sheriff doesn't seem to be very concerned about it.

Matt finally got the inside scoop that he was looking for. A townswoman was leaving town and she knew enough incriminating information on Henry and she told him. She was leaving town for a faraway place and she wanted to clear the slate before she left. Matt was quick to react and the Innocent gang was never very far away. Henry was trying to play it cool and Matt was on to him. It was an unspoken situation, understood by both of them the last time they saw each other. The Innocent Gang was on the alert and ready for trouble. When Matt started to make an arrest, Henry and his gang were on his trail.

Plummer was in deep trouble. It was kill or be killed at this point. Matt went to Henry's house to arrest him and a fight broke out. Matt had a list of names for the whole gang at this point. The Judge and his men were already on the road and they were going to show up in the next few hours. Henry was taken into custody and held at the local jailhouse where his desk as the sheriff was only a few feet away from his cell. During his time in jail, Henry begged for mercy and he surrendered. The state lawmen were everywhere in town. The Innocent Gang was on standby but after Henry Plummer was sentenced and hanged, the Innocent Gang left the area and didn't return.

In this event, the outlaws and organized crime leaders didn't win. The list was released and several of the gang members were arrested at a later time. January 11th, 1864 is when Henry Plummer was hanged. The town of Bannack was free once again. The criminal activity was down to a very low and dole-like tone. The law stayed in the area for some time, threatening to arrest all the gang members if they didn't leave. Gold mining went back to normal and businesses were able to make a profit. Does crime pay? Maybe for a short amount of time, at least for Henry and his gang.

Many people believe that a lot of the money from the robberies is still buried and hidden in the area today. The town itself still stands today and it's now a state park with buildings still standing. If the treasures are still out there, they won't be within the town's limits. They would be in the outskirts of the area, waiting to be discovered. I'll get more into the treasures of this area at the end of this book.

SEVENTEEN

King Fisher the Texas Gunslinger

I want you to consider that not all outlaws were famous enough to have their own Hollywood shows and movies about them. Here's another thing. Not all movies, legends, and stories are facts. Think of it like the kid's game we all played. Kids sit in a group and one person starts out whispering in the ear of one kid and then it gets passed around the group one by one. The Telephone Game. Stories of gunslingers, robberies, and murders back in those days were very much like this game. By the time the message comes around and is told by many, the message is misleading and sometimes even wrong.

This happened a lot and it still happens in today's world. Did you know that many witnesses of a crime scene are only around twenty-five percent correct? That means many of the criminal's descriptions are very misleading. So think twice when you see a sketch drawing from your local police department. It's very likely that the eyes, ears, hat or no hat, the color of the criminal's hair, and the body type are wrong. Studies have been done about the memory of the person that has been involved with trauma or witnessed something horrible. It's been proven that multiple people remember the situation differently.

Let me give you an example. Eight people are in a bank and the robbers come in, holding guns. The robbers say "everyone get down." The robbers then grab the guard and hit him over the head with their pistol. Then two of the robbers go to the bank manager and ask for the keys to the vault. Three of the robbers stay in the lobby and watch for the police and manage the bystanders. Once the robbers get the money, they run out of the building, saying nothing to the witnesses. In this event, some of the witnesses are asked to give their statements.

Five out of the eight witnesses to the robbery give their descriptions of the robber's clothes, how many were involved with the robbery, and what happened during the robbery. The chances are that every one of the witnesses will give a different story and explain details that the others didn't remember or notice. Psychologists would say this could be because of the Mandela Effect. This effect is caused by false memory which occurs when multiple people incorrectly remember the same thing or event.

The reason I bring this up is that I believe this happened a lot in the old western days. Just imagine being on a moving train, it comes to a halt, and outlaws board it. You're sitting in your seat, hearing the yelling in the train car ahead of you. Your heart is pumping and your nerves are in fight or flight mode but you can't move. Do you think you will be able to obtain the whole story correctly? Science says, most likely not. We all know about the big fish story too. Some people like to tell stories grander than what really happened.

There's also the Hollywood effect and show business. These very smart writers, producers, and directors know what's entertaining and what's not. Now that I have your attention, consider all these things that I've mentioned and ask yourself, did all the western outlaws do exactly as what was told? How about the not-so-famous written-about outlaws? Do you think they were not as great as the outlaw before them? One more thing to consider. The media. If the story can be told in a way that hypes it up, the media will embellish it. They did it back in the western days and they do today.

Let's go into detail on a Texas gunfighter that was not written about as much as some. Many Texans say today that he was the real deal. A truly fast gunslinger from the west. A force to be reckoned with and to be feared. He could beat anyone in a gun draw. I'm talking about John King Fisher, the outlaw. I'll refer to him as King Fisher or Fisher in this chapter. His story starts out in October of 1853. He was born in Collin County which is north of Dallas Texas. This was the first outlaw that I couldn't find any information about his parents.

I'm not sure what that means other than, his family history wasn't written. They may have been immigrants from a different county. In fact, a lot of his history was not mentioned and I'm going to tell his story the best that I can. To me, it seems that Fisher was conflicted during his life. He was an outlaw that turned into a lawman, then possibly back to a short life of crime. History says that he changed his name to "King" because he was a flashy dresser. He felt that the name change went along with the clothes he wore. Another thing about Fisher was that he was as good with horses as he was with fist fighting.

He was good at both according to his history. He would capture wild horses and break them, and then sell them at a good profit. This was a way he made money when he was in his young stages of teenage to young adulthood. At this time, people in the area thought he was a good-looking man, with muscles, and he had the face that people liked. Almost trustworthy you can say. During this time, he was arrested for his first offense. He was caught by the local law, stealing horses. Perhaps tracking down wild horses was harder than stealing good broken-in horses. The story goes that he was finally caught and arrested and brought back to the person's house he stole the horse from.

When the law approached the horse owner, he decided to not press charges against Fisher and the law let him go. Some say that the horse owner helped him escape and the law didn't release him. Some even say that the horse owner slipped Fisher a pocketknife, which allowed him to cut the rope around his hands and that's how he escaped. I can't confirm or deny either story. Fisher doesn't have a long list of history. I can only tell you what I was able to dig up. This wasn't the first or last time Fisher got into trouble. His family was reported telling the local townspeople that he was a good boy.

They claimed that he must have been involved with others that influenced him to do bad things. Fisher was arrested again on October 5th, 1870. This time he was sentenced to two years in the Texas State prison. That prison life didn't last long for him. He was soon released in February of 1871 because of his age. He was sixteen years old when he was arrested. What happened next in his life was how I think he became a good gunfighter. It's said that after he was released from prison, he rode south to work for a rancher and horseman that hired him to break his horse in.

Fisher did this for a while, but his new job brought him new possibilities. Fisher was constantly surrounded by cattle rustlers, desperados, and tough bandits. This is the common type of hands that were hired in this type of work. Fisher became friends with some of them and as they got to know each other more, the criminal acts started to begin. Fisher thought of himself as a good dresser and when he started to make even more money, his clothes became even flasher.

It was said that he was looking more and more like a cowboy. Not the modern day cowboy but a Cow Boy from the old west. If there's a space between the word Cow Boy, that meant an outlaw or bandit. It could also mean that he liked to look good for the ladies. The town mentioned that he was a good-looking young man. Dressing like this could attract a woman or two. That's what he was becoming. He was wearing silk shirts and tiger skin chaps.

He would wear a set of holsters with silver studs on them and he had the ivory and nickel-plated six shooters to go along in them. His dress attire and his reputation were growing in town. This led up to his first gunfight which ended with him being killed. Fisher had a bad temper at times and this was one of the reasons for the shooting. He got into an argument with three cattle rustlers and he drew his guns faster, killing three of them. Fisher was left in a predicament because he killed these men. They happened to be a part of an outlaw gang in the area. After they were leaderless due to Fisher, he was appointed their new leader.

Now that Fisher was the leader, this gang started rounding up cattle, and sometimes they would make off with over one hundred head of cattle from one rustling job. He started to make the gang some good money. One thing for Fisher was, if there was any trouble, he would pull out his gun to settle the disagreement. This made him a better gunslinger every time. He was getting into so many gunfights; he was gaining not only a reputation but he was getting quicker withdrawing his guns.

Fisher was like many outlaws I've written about in this book so far. These outlaws were somehow able to avoid convictions for many of the crimes they committed. That was Fisher as well. He was arrested several times by Texas Rangers Leander McNelly and Lee Hall. Every time they thought they got their man, Fisher was released. He and his gang even got off on self-defense disputes.

Even on June 4th, 1876, Fisher and nine of his men were once again arrested and this time they were taken to Eagle Pass to stand trial. Many people thought for sure they were going to hang out not only for their recent murders and crimes but for the past too. That didn't hold up in court and they were released. Over and over again this happened. Fisher and his men were getting away with cattle stealing, robbing, and murder.

Let me give you a good idea of how Fisher was to kill people. One night at a saloon, a man refused to buy him his drink. That was a mistake that that man would never be able to change because Fisher k shot and killed him, in cold blood, right there at the saloon. Everyone there saw it happen. Fisher put three bullets in this man. This was how bold and outlaws he had become. Oh, and don't forget about the time that Fisher caught some bandits stealing his horse.

Fisher caught them hopping on top of his horse and he ran towards their direction, he grabbed one of their guns, and shot the three bandits right where they stood. Another thing that Fisher had going on for him was the fear that the townspeople would grow to feel towards him. If Fisher was arrested, not one brave soul would testify against him. Word around the area was that Fisher couldn't be prosecuted and if you testify against him, he'll come back and kill you. Fisher truly was a force to be reckoned with. No one wanted to stand up to him.

I think in his case, marriage and a family were best for him. In

1876, he did get married, and he started to settle down in Texas. He wasn't running around and causing trouble like before. Fisher still had that look in his eye and none would dare to bring up his past. Fisher was starting to get embarrassed and angry at himself for all the wrong he did in his time. Family life changed him, and he didn't want to talk about anything but the present and the future. In 1881, Fisher was in court, trying to right his wrongs.

With a good lawyer and presentation, He was able to get the court system to clear him of all his past crimes. He was a free man now. He wasn't pursued by the law and he had a chance at a fresh start. What he did with it was up to him. Around this time, law and order started to sweep around the west. Towns that were lawless were soon getting marshals and sheriffs in the area. The state was hungry for some men that weren't afraid of taking down criminals.

The lawmen in those days, had to be as tough as the outlaws they were arresting. During the same year, he was cleared of all charges, he was offered a job working as a Deputy Sheriff of Uvalde County in Texas. The law needed someone like him. As long as he was fighting for them, they figured he could clean up the area. In this case, the state of Texas was right. Fisher made many arrested and many of the outlaws feared that he would use his guns to bring them down. Some tested him and some died by Fisher's gunslinging skills.

This time, he was the law. According to history, the state of Texas may have turned the other cheek on some of his ventures. He was making a great deal of arrests and the area was slowly starting to become a better place to live. People around Texas said that he was a great lawman. Fisher was a man that may not have been able to help himself. One day, he and another gunslinger named Ben Thompson were in San Antonio. Fisher and Ben were in the wrong place at the wrong time.

That night, Fisher got the end of someone else's gun. Ben and Fisher were in an argument with the owner of the theater they were at. I'm not sure if this owner caught Fisher and Ben by surprise but he was able to kill them both. Some say that Fisher was too confident by this time. He was used to people backing down from a fight.

Maybe the owner is waiting for the right moment. Maybe he was a better shot. That I can't discover by using history but I can tell you the next day, Fisher and Ben were buried in that town. Fisher was thirty years old and Ben was forty. Texas later called this event and shooting of the "Vaudeville Theater Ambush." Later, Fisher was also known as "The Terror from Eagle Pass." He was buried with his famous chaps and flashy clothes at his ranch.

In 1930, his body was moved and reburied in Pioneer Cemetery in Uvalde. Today, you can find it and see it for yourself. Even though Fisher wasn't in western movies like some of the other famous people, he is known as the gunslinger that was forgotten. Some of the local Texas historians and western enthusiasts still remember him. They claim that he was the fastest and deadliest gunman of his time.

It's too bad he lived the previous life that he did. He made a great lawman and he was one of the good ones that started to release Texas from all the crime and outlaws.

EIGHTEEN

Exploring Ghost Towns of the West

An old homestead found by the author in the middle of
nowhere

This section of the book intended to get you locating and exploring towns of the west. I'm not going to mention well-known tourist attractions that can be found online or in a basic ghost town book. I want you to find and make some great memories and hopefully, great discoveries. These old towns are on their last leg. I know. I've explored and visited many in my time. I'm always looking for new ones that I haven't been to.

Standing in a place that was living and striving back in the 1800s is something that I can't explain to you. You have to experience it for yourself. I've walked old, uneven boardwalks of many downtown ghost towns and tried to envision what it was like back in the day. To walk, touch, see, and find things from old western history is my favorite thing to do. I will never stop exploring these types of places and I want to share that with you.

These old towns were mostly mining towns and settlements. Some of them don't have a grand downtown with hotels, saloons, jailhouses, and general stores. Some of them are places so off the beaten path, that time has forgotten them. Some of these places are only visited by local people visit them here and there to escape modern day life. If you're looking for a tourist town that you can drive to in a car, get out and walk the streets, this section is not intended for you. Those are places that you can find by doing a quick Top Ten Ghost Towns to visit on the internet.

If you want the opportunity to see and find things that are not so easily found, you must go where many people don't dare. I've visited many known tourist ghost towns and made discoveries on the outskirts of town. You can still choose those locations but become an adventurer and wander on the dirt side road outside of town. Walk down that old two track trail that's leading you into the wilderness. Then and only then will you see things the way they were left so many years ago.

Some of my best memories and discoveries have been from exploring old roads that have no street names. Places that are not on modern day maps. That's the best thing that I've learned to do yet. I can stay all day in these old mining towns. There are tons of things to see. Old mining mills, vertical and horizontal mines, relics and artifacts, and so much more. I have learned that the more I walk around, the more I find. The possibilities are endless. Even at some locations that many people do not talk about.

These pictures of this chapter are examples of what you can find. Even though I mention that history is disappearing and so are the structures, it's still well worth seeing and exploring these places. Western states are mostly what I've explored but you can find old abandoned western places in every state of America. Many YouTubers get a lot of views and make some good money from ads by filming their adventures in places like this. People like to see what they don't usually see.

An old, abandoned mine found by the author

The history is rich. Now that you're closing in at the end of this book, you should have a good idea of the western stories and legends that have been passed down for many generations now. I've traveled all over the western states to find places that I'm about to show and tell you about. I like to camp under the stars close by or I rent a hotel room in the earliest town. I like to stay more than a couple of hours in these places. If you leave early, you are only cheating yourself from adventure.

I know that metal detectorists like to hunt these places. Most of them have had visitors before you but don't let that stop you from going out and exploring. There's no way that people before you have found and discovered everything. Trust me and I know. I've put that into motion and tested to see if I could still make memories and discoveries by exploring places that are said to be hit by treasure hunters before me.

I've chosen to list the following ghost towns below due to my research over the last twenty plus years. These are places that I've visited and some of them are still on my bucket list. There's places that either hold a historical value and or are places that I wanted to see for myself. Many of these places have a huge potential for discoveries or are great for photography and memories. This list will not steer you wrong.

I've seen many blogs and read many books that I followed in my younger years. Some of them were great places to visit and some of them were not at all. These places will take you into the wilderness, looking for an adventure. You will have the chance to be in a place that truly was an area of old western history. Several of these places are towns where many of the outlaws and lawmen I wrote about in this book have been. Some of them lived in these towns or committed a robbery and more.

If you want to see the old west for what it was and still stands for, follow my list of places to visit. If you have a truck and camping trailer, you may want to plan accordingly. If you have a four wheel drive truck or SUV, I would recommend taking them to these locations. If you have an ATV or UTV, bring them. Bring your camping gear if you want to stay for a couple of days. Some of these places have motels nearby and some don't have any hotels for miles and miles away. Please find these places on the map and plan your trip to your liking.

Be safe out there and I hope you follow this list of ghost towns. Stay open minded and look for openings in the trees. Watch for outcroppings and mine entrances. Look for the old concrete and rock foundations. This is a great opportunity to get out there and find some old western history.

I've put that to the test and have found plenty after someone has hunted it before me. It all depends on the hunters experience, the hunt equipment they were using, and how good they are by using their eyes. I think you can appreciate this and I feel that you will really enjoy making some discoveries and memories of your own.

I'm going to use this chapter to list all the western states. I'll then list the mining and ghost towns in that state. I'll also leave a small description of the area's content and location.

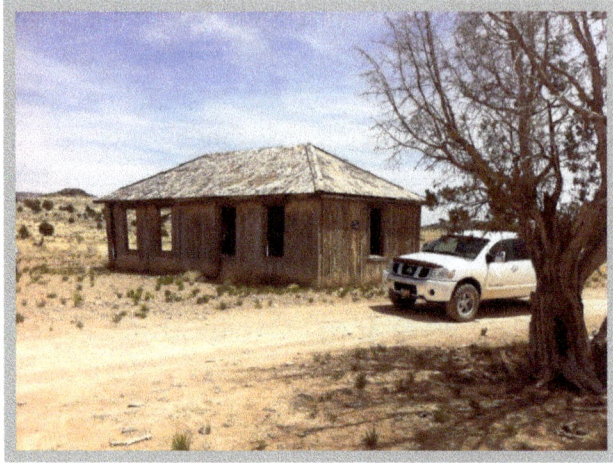

An old miners' home found by the author

This will point you in the right direction. Sometimes later, I'll write a book about eastern states and their ghost towns. Another thing to consider about chasing after these locations I mention. Some of them you will be able to get by regularly with no problem. For some of them you will need a four-wheel drive to enter the area before you can see the townsite. I suggest that you take this into consideration and do your homework before you leave your home. Look into the area and see if it's fit for you.

Places consider that you need to stay hydrated and eat while you are on your journey. I mention this part of exploring life and how to stay healthy in my book called "Legends of Old". It's a great guide to help you understand and find the equipment you need and the dangers of exploring. I've had heat exhaustion and dehydration many times in my life from exploring. I've been lost and I've had a lot of near-misses that could have ended in death. Please understand that sightseeing is much different than going out and finding these old places.

It was hard for them to live there in the old days and that has not changed at all. This list can and will take you into some hard to reach areas. Consider keeping a vehicle full of gas. Take plenty of water and food. Don't forget about first aid kits, flashlights, and camping gear. Think like a boy scout and be prepared. You'll thank me one day when you need to practice this. One more thing, make sure you bring a spare tire and tire repair kit, you're going to need it sooner than later. I guarantee it.

CALIFORNIA

Bodie Ghost Town

Is in a California State Park but it is very well worth going to. This town has a lot of history and many old structures still standing. I've written about this place many times and if you like ghost towns, this may be one of the best to see. It's protected and all the contents still remain inside many of the buildings from the original residents. If you want to see a ghost town in conditions it left, this is the place. You can drive a normal vehicle to this location. It's close to the California - Nevada border. The closest modern day town is Bridgeport California. Bring your camera!

Locke Semi Ghost Town

Is an old western town with tons of original buildings. This is another easy to get to ghost town and it's so well preserved that I wanted to list it. It's located south of Sacramento. You can find a place to stay at a hotel and you can visit and admire it. I'm very surprised at the way the town looks today. It's like walking down the streets of an old western town. This place gets many visitors so you'll blend in very well.

Calico Ghost Town

Is a great place to visit if you're passing through on the highway of the Mojave Fwy. It's just east of Barstow, California. You do have to pay to get in but I think you'll like it very much. It's quite large and there's plenty to see and do there. It is a Regional Park. It's open all year round and it's only closed on Christmas day. It's a restored old western town for everyone to enjoy. They have hotels, RV lots, and campgrounds for you to stay in. There's a museum, a mine tour, gold panning, and so much more. It's truly a fun place to see. They even have places to eat there.

Dublin Gulch Cave Dwellings

In the 1920s, miners and mining companies wanted to remain to mine the area but they had a hard time with the summers. The residents' budget didn't fit for lumber and delivery so many of them took to the nearby hills for shelter. They dug out homes into the hills there. The homes have chimneys and doors. This is truly a site you will not want to miss. There are no residences in the area. There's a cemetery and plenty of these cave-like dwellings to explore. The location is near Shoshone, just off Hwy 127 and Hwy 178 toward Pahrump. A two-wheel drive is all you'll need.

Clair Camp Mines and Structures

This area served as a mining camp and started in 1896. Over a million dollars worth of gold was mined in this area and over two hundred miners lived there at its peak. It was considered a small town rather than a mining camp. This town didn't last more than a couple of years. Too many miners were trying to work there. It was successful in its time and homes were built, wooden mills were constructed, and heavy mining equipment was brought in. The mine can still be discovered along with tons of old artifacts from the old days. Many abandoned cars are found on the side of the road, leading to Clair. This is a rough road and you will need four-wheel drive. Even then, the road is impassable at the top. Buildings are still standing and there's much to be seen.

Benton Mining Town

If you're a person that wants to explore tons of mines and see the remains of an old west mining town, this location is for you. Many of the original buildings are still there. They're in bad shape much like other old towns. Mining artifacts and iron objects can be found all over the area. The cemetery is something to see too. This town was started in 1862 and it continued on until 1889. There's plenty of sightseeing and treasure hunting to do. If you want to explore mines, the nearby mill is called Bling Spring Hill or Yellow Jacket Mountain and it is covered with abandoned old mines.

This sounds like a place that would be good to camp for a weekend and explore during the day. The modern day name for this area is Benton Hot Springs. Once you get into the mining town, you'll need a good four wheel drive to get you around the outskirts looking for mines. These are very old wagon trails leading up to them.

Coloma Mining Town of the Gold Rush

This is also a very famous town for the gold rush era. Coloma is just North of Placerville and this area was home to thousands of miners looking to strike it rich. It was started in 1848 and it had over three hundred wooden framed buildings and a large hotel. Because this palace was so remote, it cost miners an arm and a leg for any type of supplies. All you need is a two wheel drive to get to this location. If you want to see more than the average Joe, you'll need to stay on the outskirts of town in the nearby mountains. This town is on many people's lists to see.

Nevada City Mining Town

This was the largest mining town ever recorded in California. It hit the peak of over ten thousand residents. It was a thriving gold town. By 1850, Nevada City had over two hundred and fifty buildings in its town limits. Businessmen and miners made their money here and this place today has no shortage of an old western attitude. This is a semi-ghost town because there are still residents that live there today. I recommend that you look into the side roads of the area. Look for the smaller mining camps and mines. This is where you could make some really good memories and discoveries. You only need a two wheel drive to get to the town.

OREGON

Sumpter Mining Town

This town is perfect for the tourist that wants to see a great mining dredge. There's a museum to visit and the walk through town would be a great idea. This town still has the spirit of mining in it. They get many visitors every year. Nine million dollars of gold was produced in this area and the town hit a climax of two thousand people. If I was you, I would visit the town and tourist attractions but after that, I would head for the hills. Do some exploring and track down some of these old mines. You only need a two wheel drive to get to this location.

Greenhorn and Canyon City

These two towns were small mining towns of the early gold mines. Greenhorn never grew too large and today, there's a few old buildings and abandoned mines in its area. There are no tourist attractions to see here. But the scenery is beautiful and it sits around six thousand feet in elevation. Canyon City is about an hour away so if you would like to hit both towns in one day, I think it's safe to say you could do that. Both towns have a lot of western history and it's very much worth the trip. You only need a two wheel drive to get to these areas.

Granite Mining Town

This old townsite was a booming town with over five thousand people living there during its peak. The area still has a few residents living in the area but it's pretty much considered a ghost town. There's still some great old buildings standing and a cemetery. This town had a total of two thousand, one hundred, and twenty two mine claims in the area. I think it's very safe to say that if you would like to visit it and take a look around, you could see some really cool stuff. I know that mining towns with this many mines makes for a great adventure. There's still some old buildings still standing. The mines are not too far away.

Homestead of Hells Canyon

This was a mining town that was built in the 1800s. Many standing buildings are still there today and there's no residents in the area. Because of the price drop of gold in the 1900s, this place was abandoned and forgotten. Today, I think you would really like the scenery and enjoy the hunt. Many mines are in the area and two of them were very wealthy mines. There are some really great homes still standing with craftsmanship that you have to get pictures of. There's a school house, and more that will blow your mind.

WASHINGTON

Bodie Mill Town

This town was started in the early 1900s and its primary purpose was to mill wood. It had a post office, a general store, and a hotel. The mill produces a lot of lumber for the mining towns in the area. It still has a few buildings left standing but I think exploring the area and doing some scouting would be best at this location. If a metal detector could be used, I'm sure that you can find all kinds of things there. Once you're in the area, you should explore some of the mining towns nearby. It'll be worth your time and a great adventure.

Molson Mining Town

This was just a couple of miles south of the Canada border. The town is more of a small attraction place for visitors but what is still in the nearby mountains is the treasure. The population only got as high as five hundred people but it grew to those numbers overnight. The town location is on private property so be on your best behavior. You only need a two wheel drive to get to this location.

Nighthawk Supply and Mining Town

Nighthawk was an early built mining town that not only had many mines, but it also acted as a trading and center point for supplies coming in and out of the area. The town was connected with the main route with a bridge that went over the nearby river. On the other side of the river is where you will find the mining claims. Many of the buildings are still standing which include a hotel, mining buildings, a brothel, and more. I think someone would not only like this area for its history, I think there's a huge potential for exploring and finding things that no one has yet. If you really want to make a discovery, stick to the top of the nearby mountain and there's where you will find many mining cabins, ruins, and more.

ARIZONA

Tombstone Silver Town

This town is a tourist attraction but this is a great place to see what the old west was like in its wildest times. This place gets a ton of visitors and it's thriving for sure. You can stay here for days with the events and guides they have here. You can take mine tours, visit museums, and even eat and have drinks at the saloons. There are hotels in town and some are just out of town. If you're going to visit a ghost town attraction, I suggest it to be Tombstone. Home of the famous stories of Wyatt Earp, Doc Holliday, the shootout at the OK Corral, and much more. This is one of Arizona's most popular places to visit for western history.

Goldfield of the Superstition Mountains

This is another tourist attraction but you have to see it. The landscape is home to the famous Lost Dutchman Mine in the Apache County area. The owner of this town has done a great job with making it as fun as he can. There are stores, gift shops, mine tours, and more to do here. The owner of this town is very knowledgeable about the mining history in the area. You will not be disappointed if you visit here.

Tip Top Silvertown

This location is not a tourist attraction. You will need a four wheel drive to get there. Many of the old buildings are decaying away but the foundations and mines are still there. This is a much less traveled area and if you're looking for a glance at the old west, this is a place to go. Explore for mine opening and be careful. Many of the buildings were made of stone.

Oatman Gold Town

Oatman was truly a wild west town. The area today invites everyone that wants to learn about it. This town was started in 1863 and it saw its share of outlaws and bandits. It produced more gold than many towns in the west. At the peak of its time reached around thirty five hundred people. You can still find the old mines in the area. If you're driving on Route 66, this is one of the highlights to stop.

Ruby Ghost Town

This is one of the most preserved ghost towns in Arizona. Many of the buildings are still standing and it is a sight to see. It's very close to the Mexico border and there's a lot of history to it. History says that the Spanish came from Mexico territory and called this place "Oro Blanco " which stands for light colored gold. This booming mining town had its outlaws and shoot outs too. I would suggest if you're very in the area to go see it. If you're a true adventurer, visit the main part and then go to the hill from there. Mines and artifacts should be found here. The museum there had some great artifacts from the mining era.

Prescott Metro Area

This is a modern day town with a lot of history but something has even more history then the town, the area, and the outskirts of Prescott. If you look and research to the southeast and west, you'll find many old towns. This area is rich with outlaws and bandits. There's so much about this area, I'm thinking about writing a book about Arizona and most of it will be about this area. Look for old towns like Gold Bar, Oro Grande, and Jerome as mining towns but there were also a lot of stagecoach towns, supply towns, and resting towns. This area of Arizona is something that you'll want to check into.

NEVADA

Pioche Silver Town

This was a wild town and many outlaws and bandits stayed in the area to further their criminal life. I wrote about this town in the book and it starts on page fifteen. Miners couldn't feel safe at their mines because of the looting and murders committed here. The town is an attraction today and you can get there by two wheel drive. You can book a room at several hotels and there's serval places to eat. The town itself is great with a lot of wild west history. In the nearby hills, you can go exploring for old mining structures and mines themself. You would not be disappointed by visiting this area.

Austin Gold and Silver Town

There's many buildings to see here and residents still live in the town. It makes it easy to get to and easy to stay. Over ten thousand miners and townspeople came to this place during the gold rush. Everyone wanted to find their fortune in mining and this was a place to do it. This town has churches, schools, hotels, stores, saloons, and more. This was a thriving town. Many claims were laid to rest once the price of gold and silver dropped. But the mines and artifacts are still around for the person that wants to find them. This town was discovered in 1862 and it's still going today.

Rhyolite The Party Town

This town had over fifty three saloons built in this highlight time. I've never heard of that many in one town. The townsite itself doesn't have a lot of buildings standing. Don't get me wrong, it's still worth seeing. There are large mines to the east and west of the town. These are huge mines that can be seen by satellite maps. The townsite is massive. It is located just outside of the Death Valley National Park. It had over six thousand residents at one time. It was started in 1905. At one time Paramount Pictures took over the town and used a couple of the buildings in films. There's a lot of ground to cover in the area.

Delamar Silver Strike

This town is way off the main road from any normal traveling but that's why it would be a great place to explore. It's worth the drive and many old buildings are still standing. It started in 1890 and it quickly boomed from there. Assays were reported from as small as seventy-five dollars per ton up to one thousand dollars per ton. That's a huge find considering that seven-five dollars in 1890 is worth about twenty five hundred dollars. If this place still had silver, a person could make a great living reworking this place. Most of the buildings are made of stone and a lot of mining equipment can still be found.

Marietta Salt Town

Salt and borax was discovered in this town in 1867. This area was consistently robbed by outlaws. Thirty times in a short amount of time. This made it hard for the area to prosper but the town made it through it. There are still many stone buildings like homes and stores still standing today. There were thirteen saloons, a post office, several stores, and many stone and adobe huts built in the area. Today it's mostly dead but some residents still live there. You only need a two wheel drive to get there and I think you would be glad you did.

White Pine County

I'm not even going to try to write about every ghost town in this county. I think there's close to, well it's over fifty townsites. This would take a book for just the county alone. Some of them are small towns and some of them are big. Some have no remains of buildings left while some do. Do your homework and research this area before you go heading for the hills. Bring your four wheel drive and everything you'll need because you've going to need it. This is a huge gold and silver area.

UTAH

Frisco Silver Town

This is a remote but great place to visit. It's also close to Minersville and Shauntie mining areas. I've explored all three and there's a lot to see. Some of Frisco is on private property. Stay away from that area. If you go to the main downtown area, there's only rock remains of foundations there. This area was a very rough place in Utah at the time. It was lawless until the new sheriff came and threatened to shoot any outlaw, bandit, or criminal. There's also four kilns there. If you visit Newhouse, relics and artifacts can be found like a junkyard. They are everywhere. There's serval mines in the area to explore. I suggest you stay close to Newhouse or go to the North of Frisco. Bring your four wheel drive.

Leads - Silver Reef Town

Silver Reef is a place that seems at first, to not have much. The history is rich and this is one of the only places where silver was discovered in sandstone. Mines can be found all over the area. The town is starting to take form in history and there's a museum that you can visit. The staff is very nice and friendly and they know a lot about the area. Fun place to visit. There's another small mining town to the east called Babylon. You can find some stone foundations and many mines there too.

Gold Springs and Stateline Towns

Gold Springs is a very remote place and only some hunters during the season really travel here. I've had it on my list for a very long time now. It's going to take four wheel drive to get there. Keep your eyes out from mine dumps and mine openings. There are still a few wooden mining shacks in the area. Stateline is very much like Gold Springs. Little building remains but the mines are good and many between the two towns. Plan on having a long day of traveling or bring your camping gear. I think a person who is willing to explore could find a lot of great things here.

Eureka Ore Town

This is a semi ghost town but the buildings are very cool to see. There're many mines in the area, just outside of town. Many mine dumps can be seen from the main street of this town. It was started in 1871. During the great time of mining in this area, it reached over three thousand people. Like many mining towns, it closed its mines during the 1930s - 1940s. If you're in the area, take a drive out there. You'll be glad that you did. There's more towns to visit close by. Homansville, Knightsville, and Dividend.

Ophir Mining Town

This is a great place to visit and explore. People in this area really like the town's history. Museums, stores, and mines can be visited. Many of the old wood structures can still be found and explored. There's many mines so bring your flashlights and be ready for an adventure. Some of the locations of interest are private property so look for signs. I highly suggested visiting this area.

IDAHO

Idaho City Gold Town

This is a very fun town to visit. It's a tourist attraction but don't let that fool you. There's many prospectors and miners still in the area to the north, looking for gold. This town is quite large and you can spend a whole day exploring it. Stores, hotels, museums, and more can be found here. There's a place to learn how to gold pan and walking the main streets will be like you're in the old western days. You can get to this place with a two wheel drive.

Once you explore the town, head north to the Spanish Fork area and explore the old mines and dumps. This place is great for a family and the kids will enjoy it.

Silver City and War Eagle Mountain

This town was called the queen of ghost towns but it was the day. It's remote and many of the buildings are still standing today. The hotel and saloon is up for reservations and you can stay there. A campground can be found to the north and south of the town. I strongly recommend visiting this place. If there's snow in the mountains, I would wait until spring time to travel. War Eagle Mountain can be found to the east, on the other side of the mountain from town.

This is where I found many abandoned mines. If you travel to the west of town, you can find more mines and old artifacts from the mining era. This is a place to visit. You can use a two wheel drive to get to town but you'll need a four wheel drive to explore the mines outside of town limits.

Bayhorse Gold Town

Is a place that is decaying with time but if you would like to see old original buildings, it has several of those. This town boomed when gold was found on the nearby mountain slopes, seen from town limits. You will be able to see the old structures of the milling mills and the mine dumps as you come into the area. I strongly suggest visitors to this area. Look for fences and stay outside of them. If you want to sightsee, you only need a two wheel drive. If you want to explore the ruins and mines in the mountain slopes, bring your four wheel drive. Kilns are still standing in the area and every bit of this place needs to be photographed.

Rocky Bar Mining Town

This town was started in 1863 due to the discovery of gold in the Feather River area. It had twenty five hundred residents during its heyday. The buildings still standing are old but are very nice to see. Several buildings like the jail, saloon, store, and a few homes are still standing. The mines can be found in all four directions of the town center. If you're in the area, you need to go visit it. Two-wheel drive is all you'll need to get to the downtown section.

If you want to wander and explore the old mines and ruins, you'll want to bring a four wheel drive. You can ride old mining dirt roads heading to the north, south, and east of the town. Keep your eye out for discovery. You might want to bring a gold pan with you.

Gilmore Farming Settlement

This town served as a farming community and it's a great place to see how a normal town was created, rather than a mining town. The buildings are spread out in a section and many of them are still standing. These are mostly wooden built homesteads for the families that lived there many years ago. When the town started, people were hoping to make it rich with gold and silver but that failed early in the 1900s. There are a few really good buildings still standing and I would suggest that you visit this place. There are over thirty structures still intact but they are decaying. Old mines can be found to the west of town if you're interested in looking for them.

Burke Silver Town

This area still has residents that live in the town limits but there's a lot of old original history abandoned in this area. Silver, lead, and zinc was booming in the place and the nearby mountains surrounding the town. Many of the old mining mills are still standing. Many people have reported that the old buildings have a creepy feeling when you walk in and explore them. If you're wanting to discover mines and their ruins, drive to the north, south, and east of town and you'll see plenty. This is right on the Idaho and Montana border. If you have a four wheel drive vehicle, there are plenty of old mining roads leading to the old mines on the mountain slopes.

NEW MEXICO

Mogollon Mining Town

If you're going to be in the area of southwest New Mexico, you need to see this town. It was started in the 1870s and quickly turned into a boom town. The great thing about this area is that it's very well spread out and you could spend a whole weekend exploring. Many old buildings are still there today. Old mines can be found very easily in all directions of the town center. Some of the structures were made out of wood and some were rock, concrete, and adobe. The scenery is beautiful and the area feels very remote. I would strongly recommend visiting this place. This is a famous town with a lot of history. Even Butch Cassidy had stayed here as a small headquarters at times. Well worth the drive. A two drive will get you to the town center.

Madrid Coal Town

This town has some great history and many of its original buildings are still standing today. It's located in Santa Fe county and you'll only need two wheel drive to get there. This is a place that you have to see for yourself to believe it. There are many homes and the town limits are quite large. This town served the mining community, Many homes were constructed as this was a town for the workers and their families.

The town thrived and it had its share of many visitors. The

Spanish entered the area in the 1500s and the local Indian tribe lived here before the west was created. You have to visit this place if you're in the area. You won't be disappointed. If you're looking for a tourist attraction, visit during the summertime.

Golden Mining Town

This was a place that survived and during the gold rush, it thrived even more. It's known as an old town in New Mexico. Some people started to settle and work in the area in the 1840s. The Spanish were in the area before that and the local Indian tribe lived there before that. Many old original buildings still stand in this town. Some are only ruined with their foundations intact and some are standing strong. The old church built in the 1830s is still there and many people enjoy visiting it and taking photographs. Many people say that the gold is long gone in the area and modern day prospectors do not visit for minerals.

Hanover - Fierro Mining Town

Just a few miles to the east of modern day Santa Clara New Mexico there's old mining history to be discovered. From Silver City to San Lorenzo, you can find many townsites and mining operations in the area. In fact, some very large modern day mining companies are still mining the area. Their open pit type mines can be seen from a long distance away. I would suggest that you take a good day and explore this area. Many old structures and ruins can be found. It would be well worth your time. From Bayard, take the 356 route heading northwest to enter the area.

Lincoln Townsite

If you're in the area, you have to visit the town where Billy the Kid and the Regulators resided. This is the center of the Lincoln War and the main street name is Billy the Kid. There's a museum, the old courthouse, and much more. This town is not considered a ghost town, people still live there today but it's something that I think you'll enjoy visiting. Take a stroll through this historic town. You can get to this area with any vehicle.

COLORADO

Teller City Silver

This town was discovered in 1879 because of the rich silver veins found in the area. This town grew to a huge population and there was a large hotel, twenty seven saloons, and hundreds of log cabins built here. This old and abandoned town sits around eight two hundred feet in elevation. Because pine trees were a great source in the area, that's what many of the buildings were made of. Today, you can find the log cabin style buildings spread out within the town's limits. Most of them are in bad shape without the roofs covering and protecting them. The drive in is beautiful and well worth the drive. This is a place where you should bring your four wheel drive vehicle. Explore by foot around the old town site.

Saint Elmo Gold Town

This town is named one of the most preserved ghost towns in Colorado. Many old wood structures are still standing and the residents in and around the area have done a great job keeping this place like it was back in the old days. This town was started in the 1870s and it sits around ten thousand feet in elevation. It was a thriving gold town with saloons, and a dance hall. Its population hit around two thousand people plus. Serval gold mines, ruins, and equipment can be found on the south slope of the mountain. You have to see this town if you truly want to see an old western town. Keep in mind that elevation change can affect your body.

Telluride Townsite

This is one hundred percent of tourist attraction locations and it served some wealthy people too. It's very much like Jackson Hole Wyoming but you still need to go see it if you're in the area. This town has never died but back in the day, it was a crazy rough town. It has seen its outlaws like Butch Cassidy and his gang. The Ski resorts and fancy stores make this a Disneyland-type attraction but there's more to this area than that. I would suggest spending a couple of days in town. Learn the history and see the attractions. From there, I would plan a couple more days to the east slopes of the town.

Many old mines were located there. Many people are there for the town. You can be there for both if you plan it right. I learned many years ago that this town got its name from one thing. It was hard to get to. Many outlaws hid in the town to escape the law. Saloons and brothels were entertainment. The saying is, you'll stay here in town "tell you ride," Telluride.

Animas Forks Mining Town

If you want to visit one of the highest mining camps in the USA, you need to visit this place. It sits over eleven thousand feet in elevation. If you like to hunt for mines and ruins, this place has many. All you need to do is pick a direction to explore and you'll find them. Because of the remote location, I think there's still plenty of opportunity to find some great discoveries. There are still some really good log cabin buildings and ruins of a huge mining mill. If you go off the normal path of the main road, you can find many miners cabins and the artifacts left behind. Bring your four wheel drive, you're going to need it.

Central City Mining Town

This area has a lot to see and give a visitor. If you like old mining history, this place has it all. Just by using satellite imagery, you can see that the area has hundreds of mines, dumps, and mills. This is an area where you can truly get an idea of what it was like in the old days. I would

plan on visiting this area for a couple of days. Camping would be beautiful or perhaps a hotel nearby. This area still has many residents but it's full of wilderness to explore. This area is so large, full of mines and old mining cabins, it's mostly a metro city to a couple of town limits.

Many of the mines are located to the south and southwest of Central City center. Bring your four wheel drive and do some exploring. I know for a fact you will create memories that will last a lifetime. This is a must-see area.

WYOMING

Atlantic City, South Pass, and Miner's Delight

This town of Atlantic City only lived for a short ten years but there's plenty to live and see at this townsite. The town grew to around two thousand people. Miners and businessmen were trying their luck at making money. South Pass is a town that was started in 1842 and was the home of the Sioux and Cheyenne Indians. South Pass grew over its time and by 1870 it was home to over four thousand people. Miners Delight townsite started in 1867 and was a mining town just like Atlantic City and South Pass.

I've listed these three mining towns because they are very close to each other. I would say you can spend around two to five days in this area exploring. This area is full of history. Even Calamity Jane was in this area when she was younger. Many old original buildings can be seen. Cemeteries can be visited. There's also a large open pit mine just to the north on the backside of Roundtop Mountain.

I think you should plan very well if you're going to head out to a place. Consider staying at a hotel in Atlantic City or tent camping or camper trailer in the wilderness. The landscape is pretty and I feel that if you explore and keep your eyes out for mine dumps and miners' cabins, you can have a great adventure and see many things. Bring your gold pan, and give it a try.

Carbon Mining Town

I will tell you right off the bat, there's no real structure at this location that is still standing today. All you'll find are old foundations and crumbling walls. That being said, this town is not on the normal list of ghost towns to visit in Wyoming. That makes this place more untouched than others. You can find the cemetery there and you'll see mine dump's just from the center of the ruins. I've found many relics and artifacts, including lost mines in places like this. If you're in the area or passing through, I would go and take a look.

Rambler and Battle Coal Mines

When it comes to buildings, this might not be the area for you. This town is not known for its tourist attractions and structures of the old west. This is an area not unfamiliar with mining. There are a few small buildings standing but the real treasure is the exploration of the area. This was a coal town and what comes along with that are the mining artifacts and equipment. If you're in the area or if you want to look for possible lost history, mines, and cabins, this would be a good place to start looking.

Keep to the south end of town. Follow the old dirt roads with your four wheel drive to get around. There are also some bigger mines to the west of the town center. Explore and have fun here.

Kirwin Mining Town

Kirwin still has a few scattered old buildings in this area. If you go there, find the townsite where the old decaying buildings are and also go to the south across the Wood River. I will tell you, some people have claimed this area of having an eerie feeling when you spend some time here. This is the final destination point of the road.

There's only one way in and one way out. At the end of town, there are a few miner cabins that can be found to the southwest of the town. Follow the Wood River and you'll find them. The area has several dirt trails and roads there. It would be wise to bring your four wheel drive vehicle and hiking boots. Some of the standing buildings are perfect for photographs.

Jackson Hole

If you haven't been to this town, you have to go see it. The Grand Tetons Mountains are breathtaking. The history of the area is very rich and I know that you will not be disappointed. It's close to the main route that takes you to other locations like Yellowstone Park and more. You can plan on staying in and around this area while you're traveling and exploring ghost towns. This is a modern day town and many wealthy people come here for fun. There are plenty of hotels, stores, restaurants, and much more. You'll be glad you stopped here.

MONTANA

Bannack State Park

I'm going to go ahead and say it. I think this old mining town could be the king if not the queen of ghost towns in the western states. Right up there with Bodie and a couple of others. Grasshopper Creek was where gold was found and this town soon became a booming town full of the 1860s. Thousands of miners and businessmen came to this town and area to make a living. This is a tourist attraction but don't let that stop you, this place is great. This was a popular stop for outlaws, lawmen and even Henry Plummer, he was made sheriff of this town. I mentioned him in this book if you remember.

Many of the buildings are still standing very well and this place is famous for its photography. If you go here, bring your four wheel drive and explore further out from the town's center. This was a gold rush town and many mines to the southeast of town. This is a one way in and one way out destination. If I was you, I would camp out at the campgrounds to the west of town. You'll pass it as you come in. To the north of town is a place where several mines were worked as well.

Plan your trip according to the weather and how many days you plan on staying. Explore and don't be afraid to walk around the outskirts of town. You'll never know what you'll find in a place like this.

Virginia City and Nevada City Placer Towns

This town was once the richest place in Montana for placer mining. It's now a tourist attraction that has a lot to offer. You can stay at the hotel, eat at restaurants, and take tours. Gold panning is popular here too. If you visit during the on-season time, you'll find that there is much to see and do. The original buildings have been kept up and some are restored but it doesn't take away from the adventure. Most of the mines were dug to the south of town.

Nevada City is just a very short drive from Virginia City. It will almost feel like a connected town to you. I've written a lot of history in this book about these two towns. I would make a weekend trip out of this place.

If you bring your four wheel drive vehicle, I would drive down the old dirt road leading to Bald Mountain, south of these towns. There are a lot of mines and old miners' shacks in this region. I can tell you that there's still a lot of lost history, mines, equipment, and artifacts that are waiting for the right person.

Granite Mining Town

If you're looking for a town that isn't on the normal stop for travelers and explorers, you need to plan a trip to Granite. It's located in the mountains to the east of Philipsburg Montana. Many of the buildings are just the way they were left back when the towns died. The mountain is surrounded by mines that are spread out throughout the area. Canyons and peaks reveal new structures and mining equipment everywhere you go.

Bring your four wheel drive vehicle because you're going to need it here. Some exploring by foot would be a great idea as well. Bring your camera because you'll be mad if you don't. You can stay at Phillipsburg or you can camp somewhere nearby. I guarantee you that you will not be mad that you traveled here. If I lived nearby, I would be in those mountains every weekend, exploring and looking for anything from the past.

Elkhorn State Park Silver Town

Even though this is a state park, you need to see it for yourself. It's in the vicinity of other known ghost towns in Montana. It would be the same not to see it. This place produced a lot of silver, thousands of dollars' worth every month, and back then that was a lot of money. You don't need to have a four-wheel drive to get to the townsite but if you want to explore deeper in the wilderness, you better bring it. Most of the min mines can be found to the northwest of the town.

If you're here to find lost history or you're just sightseeing, this is a great place. Some of these wood structure buildings will blow your mind. Great craftsmanship. The modern day town of Boulder isn't too far away. It's about a thirty minute drive.

Take the side roads if your car permits it. There's more to see here than just the townsite. Mines and mills are spread out everywhere.

Comet Mining Town

If you want to see a small town with many buildings still standing that are off the main route, you found it. Many old original buildings are still standing here. The mines can be found scattered around the vicinity. I would bring a four wheel drive to this area because the town is only part of the fun. South from there, over High Ore Creek, are many more mines and old mining buildings. I would explore these side roads in the area.

The wooden structures are definitely crumbling down but the town is still very much worth it. I believe I've counted over forty old buildings in this town. That's not including the miner cabins and mills on the outskirts. I believe someone can spend a lot of time exploring on foot and a vehicle in this area.

Further Thoughts, Regulations, and Laws

I've mentioned several ghost towns in this chapter now. I don't want to mislead anyone into seeing other ghost towns in these states, I just know that these are the ones on my list and I wanted to share them with you. Not all these locations are secluded from other visitors and tourists. Some are so off the main path, you may not see anyone for the whole day. Some, you'll want to leave very quickly because too many visitors are there.

I tried to find a good mix of structures that are well managed for the little mining camp that time forgot. If you were able to visit even a couple of these townsites, you would be considered a ghost town hunter and explorer. Learn all that you can from every place you visit. More importantly, do not destroy and damage any historical building, equipment, miners cabin, and really anything of the past. Some of these hidden and far away towns are crumbling not only from time but from people who have done them harm.

If you four wheel drive on a dirt road, obey the laws and stay on the main routes. The BLM and Forest Service close down areas that have been misused by outdoorsmen and explorers. Once this happens, they hardly ever open the area back to public use again. Please do not be one of those people or groups. I've been exploring places like this my whole life and I've seen many places closed and cut off.

You need to understand the state and county laws as well. Many states in America have laws that you can't take any relic or artifact that is older than fifty years old. If you make a great discovery, you're required by law to turn it in to the authorities. Let's leave the area you visit the same way you found it. Enjoy these locations and let's think about the future and the people that want to visit it and see what you saw. If you haven't already, read The Antiquities Act. This will explain the ins and outs of the most important law of anything old and historical. Keep in mind, every state and every county can enforce additional laws.

It's important to know these laws. You can't tell the courts that you were unaware of them. It's another law. Remember that. I listed all the Western states and some of the ghost towns in this book. There are hundreds if not thousands more to visit. Some of the mid-states deserve recognition so I'll use the rest of this chapter to make a list of those. I think they're also important places to visit.

Texas

- Terlingua
- Indianola
- Fort Griffin
- The Grove

Oklahoma

- Ingalls
- Lenora
- Picher (Toxic Fuels from mining)
- Texola

Kansas

- Diamond Springs
- Alcove
- Bazaar
- Bloom

Nebraska

- St. Deroin
- Angus
- Antioch
- Dyson Hollow

South Dakota

- Deadwood
- Galena
- Rochford
- Keystone

North Dakota

- Temple
- Griffin
- Lincoln Valley
- Sims
- Eastedge
- Aylmer

Alaska

Alaska is the last frontier that is still wild and very much unexplored. You can find many old mining camps and towns abandoned. The Famous Gold Rush drove thousands of thousands of people to this state looking for gold. Their dreams still remain in the wilderness. Here are some places that you can visit and enjoy.

- Kennicott
- Dyea
- Unga
- Portage

NINETEEN

Outlaw Buried Treasures of the West

If you have that adventurer in you and you would like to go out in the field and find lost western history, this is the chapter for you. In all my years, I've learned that being prepared is key when it comes down to making discoveries. I would never discourage someone from going out in the wilderness, looking for an adventure. But, what if you were more prepared? If you know that area, what happened there in the past, who was involved, and what time period it happened, you'll be more successful in the field.

I left many clues and stories in the chapters above. I'm teaching you that if you understand the backstory, you can be more prepared to go find relics, artifacts, treasures, and more. If I asked you "would you like to go find evidence that Jesse James buried caches somewhere in Missouri," would that interest you? I know I would like to and it's not as hard as you may think. I've stood at many sites, finding clues that I was standing right at an area where famous outlaws and bandits once stood. I've found their relics, structures, and inscriptions left behind in rock and trees.

There's nothing I like more than to be able to find a spot where I know history took place there. Because I know the stories and legends of the person and area, I can imagine what it was like back in the day. I'll give you an example. When my team was hunting for Butch Cassidy and the lost gold of the Castle Gate Robbery, the first real clue that we found was his name, left with wagon axle grease on a rock. When I first saw it, I did my research and investigator type behavior. I inspected the name, I looked around the area, and metal was detected. I was trying to find something that may have been left behind.

When I was done with my investigation, I sat down to think. This is one of my favorite things to do. I will sit next to the clues I find and envision the past. I can picture Jesse James and his gang, sitting around the campfire while Butch was sitting in the exact same spot, writing his name. By exploring the area further, I could envision where they put their horses, I could be where their camp was. Because I knew their history, I was not only able to have the satisfaction of knowing I found something important, but I was also able to daydream about the past.

There's nothing better than that to me. I can say that I chased the clues left behind by Butch Cassidy and his gang and I tracked them to their famous Robbers Roost hideout. Once I arrived there, I found old, old, iron relics like spoons, forks, and tin cans. They match the time period and I realized that these relics were used by the gang. One of them might have been Butch's dinnerware itself. That is something that is spectacular! That's real history and discovery at its finest. You can read about him and his gang all day, but to hold something that they held, that's the real deal.

The same goes for visiting old ghost towns. The tourist ghost towns are a lot of fun. There are tours, gift shops, and shows to watch. I recommend those types of tourist attractions.

But what if you can see more? These types of towns usually are rebuilt. They look similar to the old towns of the west but they're not the original buildings. You have decided what type of explorer you are. Are you the type that wants to see what everyone can see, from the comfort of your car and hotel rooms? Or do you want to go deeper in the wilderness and find things that only a few people have seen before?

I'll give you a great story, one that I always think about from my memories. My brother, David Draper and I were hunting in southern Idaho, looking for old mines, structures, and cemeteries. We decided to take an old road that leads up to Silver City Idaho. It was spring-time and the road still had snow patches on it when the road turned around a blind corner. We were on the main dirt road that leads to Silver City downtown but we have already explored that section several times prior. This time, we wanted to find something that was not what the average person had found.

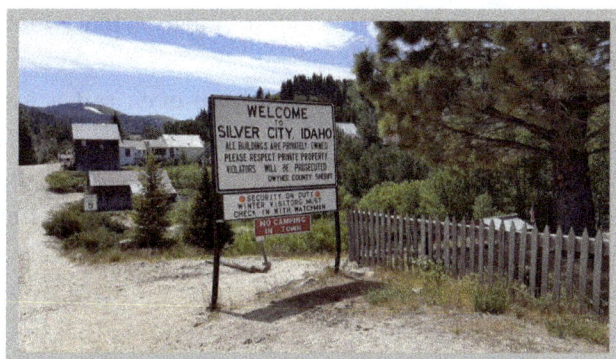

Entrance to Silver City Idaho taken by David Draper

On our way up the mountain, we referred back to a topo map of the area that was sold to us by the Hotel and saloon owner a year prior. It showed things on the map that we wouldn't have known were there unless we had that map. We inspected the map during the summer and circled a few places that stuck out to us. I was twenty-one years old at the time and an unknown adventure was driving me on. About halfway up the road, we stopped at our first area of interest. On the seven point five minute topographic map, it stated that there was a "Prospect" just off the road, about three foot-ball fields away.

There was not a good place to park my vehicle. It literally was a steep canyon to the right side of the road. I did what any good explorer would do and I placed my vehicle into a four-wheel drive and parked the car on the steep slope. My vehicle was so much at an angle, I had a good three-foot drop from the driver's seat, to the ground. I jumped out and my brother and I laughed as I tried to reach the door to close it. My vehicle was obviously not in a normal place to park.

When we used a compass and map to get our directions correct, I noticed that there was a trail and there wasn't a road heading in the direction we needed to go. We started to watch and within about two football fields away from my vehicle, we started to find a lot, and I mean a lot of iron-looking relics. There were piles of very old food cans. We found thick iron stakes and thousands of old square head nails laying around. We knew this kind of place. A place that showed no sign of traffic before us.

We inspected a lot of the relics and we even put a few in our pockets. A nail here and there and they were very old. After about ten minutes of exploring, we decided to go closer to the prospect that was labeled on the map. To our surprise, there we were standing at the opening of three mines. One mine had an old rickety wooden ladder coming out of the hole. The other two mine openings were more of a digging area. A mine that didn't go into the ground very deep. Maybe about six feet. The mine with the ladder was the one we were interested in.

We tried to go down it but it was unsafe. We wouldn't have needed to get a rope to lower us down. We spent another good ten minutes, finding tons of objects. Fabric, decade wood cut by a saw, and a lot of iron tools. Everything was heavily decadent and some of it was so rusted, we couldn't pick up the object without it crumbling in our hands. Even though we wanted to stay and look the area over better, we had an aggressive agenda for the day so we left that sight. We got back in my vehicle, which was very hard to get back in, and headed down the road a few more miles.

We have been on this road several times before, but this time we had our eyes peeled. To our surprise, we saw an old rusted car off the road. We pulled over to inspect it and once we got up to it, my brother said something along the lines of, it's an old fifties ford truck. The doors were missing and it was badly crushed. The color was pretty much red from the rust on it. It was very cool to see. My brother has always been an old vehicle admirer so he told me more about its history. As he was talking about it, I noticed a path that was on the side, about ten feet from the rusted truck.

I let my eyes wander and I noticed that it was a part of the old original road that mostly led to Silver City. Vegetation was growing over it and the tracks were old and distorted. It was the old road. New road construction slightly changed the course of the original road a little around that spot. We admired the old history and made our way further up the dirt road. We finally reached a turn in the road that we marked on the map. It was a left hand turn but it didn't look like a good approved road. It looked very rough, like an old wagon trail.

I reached down and put my vehicle into four wheel drive again and made a left hand turn. The road was awful from the beginning. The trail was about the size of my vehicle and the trees and vegetation was overgrown. The odd thing was we could tell from the cuts in the dirt and some of the tree lines that the area was maintained before but not for a long time. We travel down the rough road at about eight to ten miles per hour. I wasn't able to go much faster than that. The tree line was thick and we came up to an opening and we looked to the right. Then we noticed that we just found a very old mining mill.

The mill was in bad shape. It was barely standing up at this point. We carefully walked in the area's we dared and it was well worth it. The way this thing was built was incredible. The old iron bolts were massive and the lumber was thick. They knew how to build these things back in the day. It must have taken a lot of manpower to build this structure that was about four stories high and about one hundred feet long. We found the same type of relics again. Old, rusty, and not much to salvage. I stopped and looked around, doing a 360 scan of the area, and noticed an old wooden house, about four hundred feet from the mill.

This was what we determined as a miners cabin. The construction of it was well made and we were able to go inside to inspect it. There was not much inside but it had a rock fireplace built into one of the walls. The front door was still hanging by one hinge. This was very cool to us and I wish I could find the old pictures I took with a disposable camera that day. We stayed in the mill area for another thirty minutes or so. We wanted to see what was still there. We decided to keep following the old road to see what else we could find. We traveled the road again and about three miles later, the trees opened up once again and we saw rail tracks on the left side of the road and a mine opening to the right.

Photo taken by David Draper

We were very excited so we pulled off the road and parked the vehicle again. We walked to the left side and discovered the rail tracks. There was a mining cart at the end of it on the ground. It was on its side and had some brand and label on it. It was old and very rusty. At one We talked about trying to move it but it was too heavy. It wouldn't even bug a little. This was exciting, but we also wanted to go into the mine to see what we could find. There was no lock, bars, or anything in our way of getting in.

We walked back to the car and grabbed our flashlights and jackets. When we first inspected the opening, it looked very dark and the cool air was blowing through the opening, toward our face. We started our venture into the mine and it was dark. We discovered that the rail tracks kept going through the rest of the mine and at the end of it, there was another mining cart. We tried to push it but it wouldn't move. The mine was very damp and water was dripping from the ceiling. When we got to the end, we decided to turn off our flashlights to see how dark it really was.

We could see anything. We found a bat living inside of it but it didn't seem to mind us. It was hanging off the ceiling like it was sleeping. We finally made our way out of the mine. It was

a daily deep one. I would say that we walked about five hundred feet into it. When we got out, we scanned the area with our eyes and saw something that looked suspicious. As we were walking up to it, we noticed that it was an old cemetery. This cemetery was untouched. It appeared that many years before us, someone reconstructed the area.

It had old tombstones and newer ones present. Some of the old tombstones were nothing but rock piles. Some of them were old wood planks that were decaying badly. Some of them were head-stones that were much newer. I'm pretty sure someone in the area dedicated their respects and rebuilt some of them. Most of the tomb-stones were unmarked graves. I believe we counted over thirty or more. We stepped lightly and tried not to disturb or walk over any graves. This palace was old and most likely miners that died in the area a long time ago.

Photo taken by David Draper

We paid our respects and moved on down the road again. The adventure isn't done yet. We came up to a large concrete pad that was about two hundred feet to the right of the road. We got out and inspected the area and found that a very large mill must have once stood at this location. The concrete pad was massive. There were old rotten lumber pieces laying around but not much of the structure was there. We found old bolts, washers, and square nuts that were huge. Some of the bolts were around three feet long and about one or two inches in diameter.

We were disappointed because this was one of the sites that seemed to be tampered with by man. The others seemed to be untouched. We walked around the area for some time. We weren't finding anything. We were about to give up but about a half mile to the northwest of War Eagle Mountain.

208 | TIMOTHY DRAPER

Near the mill, we found a rooftop that was hiding in the thick trees. Now pay attention to this, you'll like it. I apologize for no pictures. The disposable camera was misplaced and back in the late 1990's you still had to develop your film and wait a few days to get it. Many of my disposable cameras were lost and misplaced over the years.

We walked up to the old wooden cabin and found that the front door was shut. The cabin was very old but somehow it seemed to be in decent shape. We expected to find a lock on the door but there wasn't. I pushed the door a little and it seemed like it would open so I pushed harder. Once we got it opened, we saw something that I've not come across very often. The place looked like a miner left one day and never came back. Not like he abandoned the place on purpose. It felt like he went to work and something must have happened to him. We noticed mice running away from our sight.

Right away I noticed that the bed was still there. The colors of the quilt were very faded. It has light blue as the main color. I noticed that the fabric was brittle and I didn't dare to touch it. It was like there were over two inches of dust on it. I noticed animal feces all over it too. Then we looked to the left, and the rocking chair was falling apart. It was standing up but barely. The small round dining table was there, in good condition but very dusty. On the table, I found a very yellow-looking paper.

It was a newspaper and it had the date of October XX 1901. I can't remember the date but I do remember the month and year. I tried to move it and it broke apart like it wasn't made of paper. I didn't touch it after that. There were a couple of forks on the floor. We even found a boot that was weather away and the only thing that was really intact was the sole. David and I didn't say much. It was a really weird feeling going in there and finding it as we did. David left the house after about two minutes and I followed him soon after.

We walked back to the vehicle and we talked about how it seemed like the miner didn't relocate, he didn't come back one morning. We continued on and ended up on the top of War Eagle Mountain is what the area was called. For all those years, the area has been in control of the Forest Service and David went back a few years ago and said that the buildings are no longer gone. The road has big boulders backing any vehicles from entering the area. David said it's all gone. He was disappointed because he wanted to show his family what we found so many years ago.

I told you this story because I want to let you know that no matter what you hear, adventure and discoveries are out there. When it comes to the old west, things are disappearing very quickly. It's not the weather and natural decaying, it's a man and new development that is destroying these places. From my story, wouldn't you want an adventure like this? Everything we discovered was in one day. We visited the tourist section three times prior then we decided we wanted to explore the outskirts.

I've found many more places that are similar to this story but you really have to be ready to explore. You have to be willing to travel to hard-to-reach places. Places that many people haven't been to. I would suggest that you buy a four-wheel-drive vehicle and some basic outdoor equipment. Above that, you need to be in the right place. A place that you know has a history of the past. I list a guide to the right equipment in other books I've written. These lists will help guide you to the equipment I've learned to use in the past. Old mining towns, ghost towns, and mining camps are perfect places.

I've explored many in my life and I have found many structures, artifacts, and more miles from the center of these old towns. The heart of the town has great things to see and I will always suggest exploring it but from there, expand your search. Go down the old faded trails and roads. Look for anything unnatural. If you see a clearing in the tree, explore it. Use old topographic maps from the 1990s and older. The new ones don't pinpoint many of the old mines, shafts, structures, and more.

It's mostly non-historical items these days. I'm going to help you start your search. I'll list some short descriptions and locations below so I can help point you in the right direction. Some of the listings below will be known as ghost towns. If you would like to learn about possible treasure locations and stories in every state of North America, I would suggest buying my book Legends of Old: A Field Guide to Lost Treasures and How to Become an Explorer. I list several treasures that are still rumored to be lost in every state of America.

It will not only point you in the right direction, but it will also give you trade secrets and insider scoops. I would strongly suggest it if you're looking for a good adventure book. Don't forget to use the internet for starting your search. Be careful of what you believe but it will get you started. Some of them will be harder to find and reach ghost towns. I'll also list some of the western outlaw treasure stories as well. Everyone is different. Some people like to hunt for certain things while others like to do it differently.

Let's start with treasures, stories, and locations from the legends and history I've listed and mentioned in this book. From there, I'll point you to ghost towns and then we'll go into the harder-to-reach mining towns.

Billy the Kid and the Regulators Treasure

In all my years, I've not heard of any Billy the Kid treasure legends and stories passed down by tells. I'm reluctant to say there are none because I feel that would be incorrect. In all my years of researching, investigating, and treasure hunting I've never come home empty handed. From what I know of Billy the Kid and his gang, they were on the warpath. If you live in New

Mexico, especially in the southwestern part, I think you may be able to find a lot of treasures left behind by the famous gang.

Lincoln County, New Mexico, is an obvious place to start. There has to be more than just murder and war to discover in this area from the past. Billy and his gang were moving around a lot. I'm positive that they robbed a few of Murph's business and stagecoaches and this is who they managed to live with for the next few months during the fighting. Because they were on the move and wanted men, they would have left the loot somewhere and they intended on coming back to get it.

I would start with local historians and go from there. While you're doing that, record the conversations or use email to keep them on file. This is a great story where you become a detective and investigator. I think you would be very surprised at what you come up with.

Finding old buildings and homesteads where Billy and the boys are known to have stayed would be the first places I checked. Some outlaws would keep their buried loot close by so they can keep an eye on it and protect it from other looters. I don't believe there's nothing to find. There has to be something. Even if it was an undiscovered location and hideout, that would add to their history. You can check that area with metal detectors to see if anything was left behind.

I'm not going to hide this from you, it could take years to track down newfound information but it would be a great adventure and I can say that confidently to you. Research, research, and that is right to keep researching. Start talking to like-minded people in that area. They would love to share what they know. Especially if you're doing this for research purposes. Some people call me a treasure hunter but I like using the term, historical treasure hunting and/or historical researcher. Try that. It will get you further.

Butch Cassidy and the Browns Park Treasure

Now when it comes to Butch Cassidy, history remembers his treasures and robberies. I would like for you to consider the same with all the outlaws and buried loot, history and people don't know all that there is to know. I guarantee you, after hunting for Butch's treasure myself, we found a lot of information about serval different treasures. Research and fieldwork are one of the only ways to find more.

I told you about the Castle Gate robbery but there's another one that I've kept to myself for a long time until I started to write books. Butch and the Wild bunch committed a lot of robberies. Many of these robberies were not found. People from that past time believe the gang hid a lot of their loot around the main hideouts where they stayed. Let's talk about The Irish Canyon Silver.

To the northwest corner of Colorado, boarding Utah, and Wyoming some say that there's a treasure that was hidden and stashed away by Butch Cassidy and his gang.

Irish Canyon is just east of Browns Park. This was another hideout area the Butch and his gang would go and lay low after a robbery. I also want you to consider that I spent a lot of time here. It's one of the most famous and most talked about refugees for the Wild Bunch. The next one up is Robbers Roost. The story is a little unknown but during the time my team worked with the Travel Channel, we heard from many historians, Butch Experts, and treasure hunters that Butch's hideout was in Irish Canyon.

Supposedly, the gang hid a cache of silver coins somewhere in this canyon. People told us that it was thirty thousand dollars' worth of these mint coins. Many treasure hunters have attempted to look for the coins but from what I've heard, no one has had any luck. Don't let this discourage you. I've learned that treasure hunters come in all shapes and sizes. Some have trade secret skills and are good at finding clues and many of them only get the title because they tried to look for riches.

Being in the right area is key and when it comes to this story, you need to track down the hideout first. It may be like Robbers Roost and there's not much left but you need to start there. Once you find that, you need to expand your search. Butch was known to leave clues around.

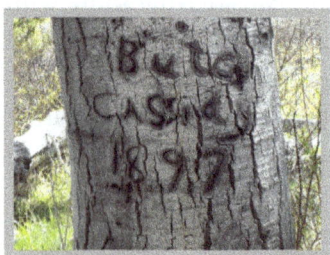

I'm not saying this tree symbol is one hundred percent authentic but this was text to me within the year after my group and I aired it on TV. I do know that we found the wagon axle grease inscription and I've heard of more in multiple states.

In every treasure story, I've chased after I've found clues left behind by the person and/or group that placed the riches there. This is when they recover their riches after abandoning it for some time. Look for any clues and anything man made. This is the number one rule for treasure hunting.

Belle Starr's Cave of Gold Treasure

Now one thing that I didn't tell you in the chapter of Belle Starr is that many local people believe that she helped Jesse and Frank James organize and plan some of their famous bank and train robberies. I cannot confirm or deny this but I've heard this many times, from many people. Throughout the years that Belle was considered an outlaw, she was involved in robberies and attacks on the Union banks, trains, and people themselves. Belle and her gang robbed a train that was transporting gold bars.

She and her gang were successful at robbing the train but this time, something was different. She was usually confident in her robberies but this time. They feared that a posse was coming after them in a hurry so they came up with a plan to stash their loot. It's said that in the Wichita Mountains of Oklahoma, they knew of a hidden cave and that's where they placed the gold.

It's said that inside the cave, the outlaws stacked the gold bars in a vertical shape, deep in the cave. I believe that the cave wasn't a big opening. This was a smaller cave with many different chambers that go in every direction. This would mean that it could be harder to reach and see the position.

One thing that seems strange to me is that people say the gang took one of the doors off one of the train cars. They dragged it behind their horses with ropes and used this iron door to cover the cave entrance behind them. People say that it's been passed down for a long time now that the door was just a support for the entrance and her group piles rocks and branches against it to conceal the opening.

If this is true, the cave entrance could be hard to find. One thing that I've experienced in the field is mines and caves that have been concealed just like this one. Depending on the terrain, sometimes the longer it's lost the rocks and branches start to crumble down, revealing the opening. Sometimes the rocks and branches get harder to find due to erosion, weather, and vegetation. It's hard to say but if you were to speak with expert cavers, they may know of some large caves in the area with small entrances.

There's one more clue and possibility to this story. In the early 1900s, a rancher and his son said that they were near Elk Mountain. They claim that something caught their attention and upon inspection of the east slope of the mountain, they found a half buried iron door. They did not investigate more but that rancher has been telling his story for years. He later heard the story of Belle hiding gold in a cave and he was certain it was the iron door he found. He was never able to find the exact location again. There's another story. It's a modern one. Whether it's true or false I cannot tell you. In 1996, a man claimed that he found an iron door in a canyon of the Wichitas. He went to a small town named Cooperton and learned of the tale sometime later.

Sure that he found Belle's iron door previously, he purchased some tools in town and headed back up to the mountains. He was found later, dead from a heart attack.

Sam Bass Hollow Tree Map at Round Rock

This treasure story includes a map that was drawn by the outlaw himself, revealing the location of a hollow tree. I would like to mention that earlier treasure hunters found the tree two miles to the west of Sam Bass Road. This area is known as Round Rock and the Sam Bass Gang did spend a lot of time there. This was the area where Sam spent his last day alive before he was found by Texas Rangers. The modern day treasure hunters cut down the tree after they located it from the hand drawn map.

They were sure that the gold was inside the tree. Man, were they wrong. The tree is now gone and those treasure hunters never found the treasure. I have good news for you if you want to continue the search. I believe that tree was only another clue of where to go from there. The gold could be buried around the tree but in my experience, the tree was used as a landmark and the loot is somewhere close by.

A hollow tree like that would have been too obvious. The outlaws must have another place nearby where the gold is. I would speak with historians and get on forums and find that information. Maybe someone still has the map or a copy of it somewhere.

I think it's safe to say that if someone wanted to spend the time and get boots on the ground, there are clues to be found. I've never found gold stashed in hollow trees and I've never seen anything but another clue on a tree. I'm sure that's the case with this story. Track down your clues, go out in the field and keep your eyes peeled for clues.

Sam Bass and his gang did keep the law bust and they had a lot of time to plan ahead. Now that I've given the true story of Sam in chapter twelve of this book, you may be able to make a discovery. Use the Round Rock as a very possible site but really use the information and locations and see if you can discover clues. Sam Bass' treasure is known that there's more than one. Some people claim that he and his gang hid several during their days of robbing.

Jesse James and the Wichita Mountain Treasures

When I first got into treasure hunting and historical research in 1997, I learned about many buried caches that Jesse hid along the trail of his robberies. Many people, for many years now, say that he hid Union gold and money in multiple locations. The Robin Hood type man he was known to be would sound right if he robbed and hid his money. It would also make sense because his targets were against the Union. He wanted to hurt their pocketbooks and bank funding.

Some say he wanted wealth and to be a wealthy man while others believe he did it out of spite and hatred for the Union. The Wichita Mountains of Oklahoma are where I would start. Some people that lived in the area during the time of Jesse James swear that he and his gang hit around two million dollars in total of gold and silver bars, and coins. The might be some clues and evidence to this. I mentioned that Jesse and Frank parted ways and Frank moved away and gave up the life of an outlaw.

After Jesse was claimed murdered, Frank did return to the area of the Wichita Mountains. It's said that he bought a hundred and sixty acre ranch. At this time, the area wasn't known as Indian territory. It was a free open range to Americans. Even though Frank's land was a ranch with cattle and more, it's said that he didn't spend much of his time working it. He hired him to take charge of that end and he spent most of his time riding his horse in the mountains.

Some townspeople say that he was spotted from a distance, criss-crossing, back and forth in many different areas of the mountain range. Rumors started to spread that Frank must have been looking for their buried loot from the years past. There's another account of Frank finding treasure symbols that his gang left as clues to recover their treasure. He discovered that the land was now owned by a widow.

The story goes on to say that he paid the widow money so he could continue his search on her land. He spent a great deal of time there looking for more symbols and clues. It's said that he found some more treasure clues that pointed that way off her land, further into the mountains. Some of Frank's friends claimed that he did find one of the treasures they buried that contained around six thousand dollars of gold.

Frank didn't give up from there. According to the same friends, he killed six horses in total, searching for the rest of the treasure within the mountain range. Frank did give up his search after seven years, looking for a strange rock formation where a much larger cache of treasure was buried by the gang. His family and friends said he very did find that one and later he died, telling about the clues.

If you ask me, this is a great story to start. I'm sure there are records of the new land that was bought by Frank and neighboring ranches in the vicinity. If you were able to really dig into the Wichita Mountains and its history, it sounds like there's something to be found. Frank looked for years and the townspeople also believed that there was treasure there. The Wichita Mountains are holding more treasures from more than one group.

In today's world, there are all types of modern day equipment to use. GRP (Ground Penetrating Radar) LiDar (Light Detection and Ranging) to scan the vegetation, metal detectors, long range detectors, and more. Many times looking for symbols carved on rocks and on trees will lead you in the right direction. There are many ways to hunt for lost historical relics and treasures. You have to decide what you're willing to do to make a discovery.

Felipe Espinosa Treasure of Colorado

Colorado isn't short of history and treasure tales. There's one I believe is worth looking for and it's involved with Felipe Espinosa and his gang. One hundred and sixty years later, there's still a treasure that hasn't been received yet. There's gold in the hills but not from natural occurrences. I'm talking about hidden gold, placed there by Felipe and his gang. Let's talk about the Park County and South Park Basin areas. Felipe and his gang rode through this area for a year, robbing and fighting their war.

This area had a huge gold strike and gold was transferred from the mines to the trains, from banks, stagecoaches, and more. Some say The Bloody Espinosas gang stashed a treasure along the main trail they used for many months. The history of this treasure is unsure of its value. Some people claimed that it was worth around two thousand dollars, while others said it was worth up to one hundred thousand.

That part I can't confirm but even if it was only two thousand dollars' worth of gold, it would still be worth a couple hundred thousand dollars based on today's gold value. On October 11, 1892, the *Rock Mountain News* reported that the treasure had to be placed in the Hall Valley area which is along the Park County Road 60. This is a good clue to tracking down the vicinity of the area. Many other news articles were written about this treasure throughout the years but there was a new, modern-day account I found.

In August 2000, an article in *Colorado Heritage Magazine*, "No Time for a Trial," claims that the treasure could be in the area of Geneva Gulch, also known as Guanella Pass. This is very interesting because the pass is named after The Bloody Espinosa's gang, Felipe's gang. They were a band of Guanella fighters in the American-Mexican war. This could be a clue. I've used many names of places to narrow down treasures I've found in the past. Especially if they're old names from the past.

There was a map that surfaced in the year 2000. It was made of some hide, skin of an animal that matches the time period of the 1860s. Some people said that the map was pointing to Felipe's treasure below Rosalie Peak, which is south of the modern day name Harris Peak and near the headwaters of Deer Creek.

I've given you some pinpoints to look into. Research and talking to people will get you closer. Due to the war matters and the murders, The Bloody Espinosa Gang's exact location is unknown. History tells that they stole the gold, headed on the trail, and didn't come back out with the gold. This is around the time that Felipe was killed by Tom Tobin. If I was you, I would look into this because Felipe and his men never made it out of this area alive. Their gold must be out there somewhere.

Henry Plummer's Lost Gold Coins

Has similarities to a modern day gangster. He was organized and he had a lot of outlaws working for him. Everything from stage-coaches, banks, local miners, freight wagons, and more were robbed in the area and he used his badge to get away with these crimes. Some say that he was involved with over two hundred thousand dollars of robberies during the mid-1800s. That would be worth well over seven million dollars of valuable loot in today's worth. Closer to eight million dollars. That was a lot of money.

Henry was hung and his gang was cleared out of the area by lawmen.

This sudden death of Henry and the posse hunting down his gang called the Innocents caused many people during that time to believe that much of the gold and silver that was robbed, would still be close to the town limits. It wasn't in Henry's bank and the outlaws arrested didn't have that money on them. The treasure must be around the town's limits, on the outskirts.

Townspeople have passed down their theory to us in the modern day. They Believe that Henry was scratching for his treasure. Many believed that he buried it around his home. History claims that a young boy saw Henry at the small creek of his property, digging on the banks. That same young boy did dig in the same area later on and found a bag full of gold coins. The treasure was a great find but it was nowhere near the amount that the townspeople thought Henry had.

From my experience, people don't pick only one exact location to bury their whole estate. There are usually several hidden locations. I think that is the case with Henry. This is a way to ensure that if someone did find his treasure, they wouldn't be able to find it all very easy.

I think that if you were able to find the location of his property line, the way it was back in the time he lived there, you could make a big discovery. A metal detector and GPR system would be perfect for this type of hunt. All you need to do is locate his property and work it. Don't give up and stay patient.

All of these stories are only stories. Nothing in treasure hunting is absolute until you find it. During this whole book, I gave you the backstory and history of many gangs and outlaws involved with possible treasures left behind. It's very important to learn the history and locations of these legends. In this chapter, I choose treasure stories that I feel have a good possibility of speaking truth and discovery.

I'm not close to these areas and it would take someone that really is devoted to finding and tracking down the information. I've been hunting for lost history and treasures for over twenty-five years now.

I can tell you that it's not easy and it's not a walk in the park. You have to be motivated and skilled in the way of taking in information and finding clues in the field. You have to get boots on the ground once you narrow down an area of interest. You can't give up either just because you didn't find it within your first two weeks.

Treasure hunting takes time. You are the collector of information. You need to understand the history. You need to talk with historians and descendants of the family members. If you can find people whose families have lived in the area for generations is a huge help as well. They usually have plenty of local known stories, legends, and history you will not find in textbooks.

I gave you the tools to further a path into exploring and historical research. I leave it in your hands to do what you will with it. I know from my experiences that one of you will not only take on the task of researching and hunting down this information, but you will make some great discoveries. It will go to the person that is serious about it and has a little luck on his or her side. I wish you luck in whatever adventure you choose and proceed in. Good luck and I hope to hear that you made a historical discovery one day.

TWENTY

My Conclusion and Perspective

After I finished my first book, *Treasures of the Ancients*, I sat around for a few days thinking about what my next book should be. I've been involved with a lot of different categories of historical research and I knew that I could choose many different topics. As I was thinking, I came up with an epiphany, I should choose something that I'm passionate about. I started my list of topics and different eras and time periods and that's when it dawned on me.

Ever since I was very young, in fifth grade I would say, I've been intrigued with the old wild west. My father, Craig Steven Draper always enjoyed watching John Wayne movies and reading old western books. My dad had a passion for old history and because he had a personal connection to John Wayne, he was naturally hooked. My grandfather, John William Draper returned from the war and was declared a war hero because of the events he encountered during the battles of Corregidor Island. Sometime later, John Wayne was hired to act in a movie called "Sands of Iwo Jima" which was later released.

This movie was partially filmed at Camp Pendleton, California where my grandfather was stationed as a Sergeant Major of the Marine Corps. Because John Wayne and the filming director's team

were there to film this movie, it's said that my grandfather was inter-
viewed and asked to help with his war experiences to strengthen
their battle senses. My grandmother, Betty J Draper-Mayne was
introduced to John Wayne by my grandfather and she was holding
my father, he was a newborn baby. John Wayne naturally wanted to
hold the baby of my grandfather, who was helping him with the
film.

You can see why my dad enjoyed watching John Wayne movies.
That one event in his life changed his pattern of interests. I was the
youngest boy of six siblings and I used to sit with my dad and watch
a lot of his movie choices in my young life. When I was a kid, I
always had a great imagination, and with that came role play in
Cowboys and Indian playtime. I always wanted to be a cowboy.
Growing up in Phoenix Arizona was surrounded by old western
history. We visited places like Tombstone Arizona and the Supersti-
tion Mountains of Apache Junction.

In my mind, I was a young cowboy and there was a time when I
didn't know the difference between the old days and modern times. I
thought I was in the old western periods from a young age. When I
was in my young teenage days, I was intrigued by horses, old
western towns, and the old mining period of Arizona. My dad and I
hiked and explored these types of places. Then before I knew it, the
wilderness was my backyard. Because of my experiences, I learned
how to camp under the stars. I was aware of the dangers of getting
lost and dehydration. My father taught me about guns and how to
shoot them.

He grew up on military bases and learned at a young age and he
wanted me to do the same. Gun safety and hunting were included in
my activities with my dad. I was a very experienced young man at
an early age. This allowed me to be more prepared for the wilderness
and I wasn't intimidated by it. I earned it. I couldn't say that all my
experiences were perfect. At the age of ten, I wandered away from
camp in the area of Snowflake Arizona. We were camping and I
woke up one morning, dressed with all my gear. I had a flashlight, a
military canteen, combat boots, binoculars, and a pocket knife.

I left our camp that morning saying that I'm going over that hill to explore, as I pointed in its direction. I paid a lot of attention to what I was exploring but I wasn't watching visual landmarks. I got to the other side of the hill and found some old relics. I spent an hour going through my discovery and decided it was time to go back to camp. During the excitement of my discovery, I lost my heading. I walked and I walked. Over one hill and then another. Within about another hour, I knew I was lost.

I was found the next morning. The summer nights are cold in the middle of the Arizona desert. When I was brought back to camp by a nice couple that found me, I was uninjured but as a young boy, I was scared. I can't tell you, I learned a lot that day. I swore to myself that I would get lost again. That didn't happen. Later in my years, I've been lost in deep canyons, large cave systems, deep mines, and more. I have luckily always found my way home. Now I use a GPS system and a compass.

I explored and enjoyed every minute I was in the great outdoors. It became a norm that I would ask my parents when the next camping trip was scheduled for the family. I carried on my days at school and home, daydreaming about my next adventure. This is very interesting because I'm now forty-three years old and I still do that exact thing today when I'm preparing for an expedition. I plan, prepare, and daydream of the possibilities coming.

When I was at the age where my friends and I retained our driver's licenses, I was the first one to speak up and mention that we should go out of town to see what we could find. Things did change in my life by the time I was fifteen years old. Our family moved to Boise Idaho and the culture and landscape were different from what I was accustomed to. The great thing about that is Idaho had a lot of mining history and ghost towns too. I explored even the mountain range I could. I started to become a ghost town hunter. I would get out the map and pick a new ghost town whenever time permitted. This carried on for years.

By the time I was twenty years old, I'd visited, explored, and researched the history of more than forty ghost towns. My drive and passion didn't stop from there. For the next twenty-plus years, I researched, hunted, and tracked down everything that was from the past. I learned that if I used history, I could find places that many people didn't know about. I wasn't able to stop there either. After attending Dixie University, I learned a great deal about finding old documents, lost history, and how to use many different sources of information.

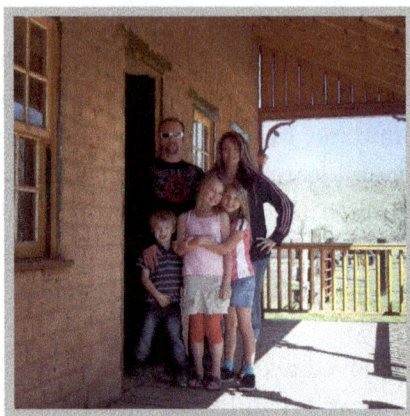

The author's family: wife LeeAnn, Jada, Trea, and Mesa Draper
—2011

I also came to realize that I couldn't just read a textbook from school to find truly lost history and sites. I had to dig deeper than the typical information that was available to the public. My life became very fulfilling and I was finding old mines from the Spanish era. I was finding old mining camps that weren't on the map. I was also learning about lost treasures and characters in history that abandon their valuables in the wilderness. The most important thing I learned from that time on was that if I wanted to know the truth, I would have to research on my own and see what I find.

To my surprise, I had over one hundred and fifty sites that were not only known by the public, but they were holding secrets. Secrets that didn't go along with the history that was being taught in the school systems. This type of history is hard to find on the internet. There are the breadcrumbs to something much different than common knowledge. I have a trade secret that I will share with you when it comes to research. Don't not and I repeat do not mix history with religion, or political beliefs, and forget what you thought you learned in school. Take what you learned out of life and discard it.

If you want to learn the truth about history, you have to go into your new search as a non-bios person. This will change everything and before you know it, your mind will open up to new possibilities and information. Remember, the history we are taught in America is controlled. For whatever reason, a lot has been hidden and even covered up. I don't exactly know why yet. I can just tell you that if you take my trade secret, you'll learn for yourself. Now back to this book and my thoughts. When I decided that I would write this book, I figured it would be as good and align with the stories I've learned in the past.

I did what I've done for over fifteen years now, I researched like I didn't know that story. I looked into my notes. I remembered my early teachings. I read many newspaper clippings and historical events. I dug into the information without a bios option. I figured that I was going to tell the story of the beginning stages of the west. How it was built, how it was involved, where the towns are located, and the bad guys that were killed for no reason. I know what I've been told and what I've seen about outlaws but a few things were sticking out.

If you noticed, all the outlaws I wrote about have their own stories. A few of them are just right down, people that did bad things but then there are the others. While writing this book, my voice started to change. My book was changing as I learned and wrote more and more. I only learned about the Civil War from school. I've only heard and read the stories about the outlaws. My options and thoughts were changing about the Union and Confederate battles. I grew up knowing that the south was wrong and the north was right.

After some time in my book, I wasn't so sure that the historical events were that simple. I asked myself, were Confederate most loyal just fighting for what they thought was right? I noticed that it became more of a cultural difference, rather than a right or wrong situation. While one party thought they were right, the other side did too. Depending on who tells the story and gives the history, it can change the reader's perspective. I noticed a lot of words such as "killer, murderer, and rebel. In whose eyes were they these things? The Union? How was the Union?

It appeared to me that the south wanted to keep the government out of their affairs. They believed that voting and culture should be agreed upon within the state they reside in. It appears the Union wanted to change that and was in a matter, forceful to make all states under one power. I know that people say the difference between the north and south was slavery. Did you notice I hardly mentioned anything about slaves in this book? That's because it wasn't coming up in my research very much.

It was in a way, not a part of what I was writing. I was able to write a whole book without getting into the confect of slavery. Yet, I was still able to write about the west, the east, railroads, lawmen, and outlaws. About halfway through the book, I called and had many hours of conversation with my dad. I think of him as a smart and fair person. I've never heard any raucous remarks from his mouth, ever in my life. He raised me to think and do the same. I had to relay what I was thinking about the Civil War and he agreed with me.

He now lives in South Carolina and he tells me that all races live together without any problems. He also told me that since he moved there, this year in 2022, he can see that South Carolina is still a strong southern state. He's reported no problems with race. I also started to see that every Confederate soldier that came back for the war was branded an "Outlaw" if they didn't change their belief system. This also seemed to push some people like Jesse James into more of a conflict after the war. I wrote this book to tell the history of each person and place I chose to write about.

I didn't pick anything based on opinion or belief. I wanted to write a cowboy story, just like if I was back in my younger years, pretending to be a cowboy. I learned a lot and I hope you did too. I hope you learned that many of these outlaws were not necessarily born bad. Many of them were placed in situations where they were pushed into this way of life. Some were bad and some felt they had no choice. Somewhere out for revenge and some were fighting for their past cultural beliefs.

Both sides of the Civil War were people and there was always good vs evil, in every group. Because I wrote this book, I don't think I can ever stop looking at western history in a different shade of light now. Thanks for reading it and thank you for considering what is in it.

I also feel that we'll consider that some of the western stories told are sometimes embellished and incorrect. I'm sure that there are many more outlaws I could've written about. Some got more credit than they deserved and some didn't get enough.

All I'm saying is, look at the history for what it is, not what someone is telling you it is. Continue reading and expanding your knowledge. Consider the possibility that you will have to change your perspective on history and the events. Stay open-minded and look for new information. Don't be quick to discard it when it presents itself to you. I encourage you to explore and become your own investigator and explorer. Find your adventure.

Image Index

Chapter 1: How the West Was Created

1: Public Domain in the USA. Mulberry St., New York, N.Y. Held at the Library of Congress Prints and Photographs Division.

2: Photo taken by the author of an old wagon from the Old Spanish Trail in Southern Utah

Chapter 2: Wildest Towns in America

1: Photo taken by the author of an old train tunnel in North Utah

2: Public Domain in the USA. Street scene of Pioche including Clark's Place and S. Thompson General Merchandise. Held at Special Collections and Archives, University Libraries.

3: Photo taken by David Draper, used with permission, of Modern-day Tombstone, Arizona

4: Public Domain in the USA. Deadwood, South Dakota 1876.

5: Public Domain in the USA. Three Pueblo Indian women displaying their ollas for sale at the railroad tracks, New Mexico, ca.1900. California Historical Society Collection.

6: Public Domain in the USA. Page 49 in *Dodge City, the cowboy capital, and the great South-west in the days of the wild Indian, the buffalo, the cowboy, dance halls, gambling halls and bad men* by Robert Marr Wright.

7: Photo taken by David Draper, used with permission, of Silver City, Idaho

Chapter 3: Mining Camps and Settlements

1: Photo taken by the author of a mining ruin's kilns at Frisco, Utah

2: Public Domain in the USA and New Zealand. Mining camp at Mount Victoria near Mount Morgan circa 1892 held at John Oxley Library, State Library of Queensland.

3: Photo taken by author of a barred up mine entrance and a "Bad Air" sign of danger in Canyon Lands, Utah Territory

Chapter 4: Marks that the Outlaws Targeted

1: Photo taken by author of a train along the Old Spanish Trail

2: Photo taken by author of an old dirt road leading to lost history

Chapter 7: Billy the Kid and the Regulator Gang

1: Public Domain in the USA. Billy The Kid tintype at Fort Sumner, New Mexico, circa 1879-80.

Chapter 8: Butch Cassidy and the Castle Gate Robbery

1: Public Domain in the USA. Fort Worth Five Photograph by John Swartz(1858-1930)
2: Photo taken by the author of the area of Robbers Roost in Southeast Utah, Canyonlands region
3: Photo taken by the author of the campsite in Goblin Valley, Utah Canyonlands
4: Photo taken by the author of Todd Andersen exploring an old miners' cabin
5: Photo taken by the author of Shaun Fotheringham at an old storage building
6: Photo taken by the author of an old Mine in the Canyonlands of Utah
7: Photo taken by LeeAnn Draper of Chris Jericho and the author
8: Photo taken by LeeAnn Draper of the author at Butch Cassidy Wagon Grease Signature location
9: Photo taken by the author of a heavy sand covered road near Robbers Roost
10: Photo taken by the author of old rock carvings/inscriptions at Robbers Roost
11: Photo taken by the author of all that is left of the Robbers Roost Cabin Ruins
12: Photo taken by the author of the Robbers Roost Corral

Chapter 10: Belle Starr the Female Bandit

1: Public Domain in the USA. A studio portrait of Belle Starr probably taken in Fort Smith in the early 1880s.

Chapter 13: Jim Miller Outlaw or Professional Killer

1: Public Domain in the USA. Portrait of James Brown Miller from the Bill James Collection.

Chapter 18: Exploring Ghost Towns of the West

1: Photo taken by the author of an old homestead in Utah Territory
2: Photo taken by the author of an old, abandoned mine
3: Photo taken by the author of an old miners' home
4: Photo taken by author of the Old Gunsmoke TV Show Town prop

Chapter 19: Outlaw Buried Treasures of the West

1: Photo by David Draper, used with permission, of the entrance to Silver City, Idaho
2: Photo by David Draper, used with permission, of War Eagle Mountain Mine Cart Tracks
3: Photo by David Draper, used with permission, of old tombstones in the Silver City Cemetery
4: Photo gifted to the author of a tree carving that says "Butch Cassidy 1897"

Chapter 20:

1: The author's family

A Look At: Treasures of the Ancients

THE SEARCH FOR AMERICA'S LOST FORTUNES

Treasure hunter, historian, and television personality Timothy Draper has one very important question for you: Will you be the one to find America's next sost treasure?

In this first book by one of the country's foremost experts, you'll gain invaluable insight into the methods used to unearth the secrets that could lead you to lost gold, silver, gems, and other hidden artifacts from the past.

Included in the book are a great number of images of clues Timothy has found while out in the field, and he tells you about how you, too, can find these clues that are all around you. He also provides a comprehensive list of known lost treasures from all 50 states to give you a jumpstart on your treasure hunting journey.

Whether you're a novice with no tools or have been a seeker your whole life with a truckload of gear, *Treasures of the Ancients* offers up valuable information that'll get you up off of the couch and into the heart of America in search of America's next lost treasure!

AVAILABLE NOW

About the Author

Timothy Draper was born in Mesa, Arizona, in 1978. At the age of 12, he developed a passion for adventure in the outdoors and history. By the time he was 18, he had already embarked on many adventures exploring ghost towns and searching for lost Spanish mines.

Timothy spent most of his adult life working in construction and venturing out in the wilderness in his free time. Later, he attended college and universities where he studied anthropology and history. He started working with film producers and major networks in 2015, and has been involved in numerous TV shows focused on treasure hunting.

In 2018, Timothy became the founder of Treasures in America, selling treasure hunting gear, and consulting with many people regarding their personal treasure hunts. In 2021, he also became the founder of the *Uncharted Expedition* web series that features real-life treasure hunting sites and situations. The show is available on many platforms.

Timothy enjoys a good hunt and spends every chance he gets in the desert or high mountains chasing after his next big discovery. He tells everyone he'll continue to search until the day he is no longer physically able to.

www.ingramcontent.com/pod-product-compliance
Lightning Source LLC
Chambersburg PA
CBHW062053080426
42734CB00012B/2637